All the things you aren't...

yet...

All the things you aren't... yet...

Jackie Humphries

WORD BOOKS
PUBLISHER
WACO, TEXAS

ALL THE THINGS YOU AREN'T . . . YET . . .
Copyright © 1980 by Word, Incorporated, Waco, Texas 76703. All rights reserved. No portion of this book may be reproduced in any form whatsoever, except for brief quotations in reviews, without written permission from the publisher.

All Scripture quotations, unless otherwise indicated, are from the Revised Standard Version of the Bible, copyright 1946, 1952, © 1971, 1973 by the Division of Christian Education of the National Council of the Churches of Christ in the U.S.A., and used by permission. Scripture quotations marked TEV from *The Bible in Today's English Version*, copyright © American Bible Society 1976, and used by permission.

The quotation on page 73 from "Little Gidding" in *Four Quartets* by T. S. Eliot, copyright, 1943, by T. S. Eliot; copyright, 1971, by Esme Valerie Eliot, is reprinted by permission of Harcourt Brace Jovanovich, Inc. Quotations on pages 91 and 129 reprinted from *The Prophet*, by Kahlil Gibran, with permission of the publisher, Alfred A. Knopf, Inc. Copyright 1923 by Kahlil Gibran; renewal copyright 1951 by Administrators C.T.A. of Kahlil Gibran Estate, and Mary G. Gibran.

The author is indebted to *A Farthing in Her Hand*, Helen Alderfer, ed. (Scottdale, Pa.: Herald Press, 1964) for suggesting some of the possible chapter divisions of *All the Things You Aren't . . . Yet . . . .* The ideas discussed in Ms. Alderfer's book prompted me to pursue them further and eventually to write my own book.

ISBN 0-8499-2891-5
Library of Congress catalog card number: 77-92468
Printed in the United States of America

To Robert—

   Because you know me
      for what I really am,
          and you love me anyhow.

Contents

Preface   9

Gifts for You

1. The Gift of Self   11
2. The Gift of the Mind   21
3. The Gift of Abilities   33
4. The Gift of the Body   44
5. The Gift of Sexuality   57
6. The Gift of Money and Possessions   74
7. The Gift of Happiness   85
8. The Gift of Time   97

Gifts to Open with Someone Else

9. The Gift of Relationships   107
10. The Gift of Marriage   121
11. The Gift of Children   138

A Gift with Which to Use All Your Gifts

12. The Gift of Power   153

Notes   159

Preface

When my husband and I were working as missionaries in Sao Paulo, Brazil, the arrival of a package from home was a happy occasion. Sometimes it came from someone we hardly knew; often it contained things we didn't seem to need; but each time we were touched. Somebody out there really cared for us! Thus, we felt an urgency to use these gifts to glorify our Lord.

Being familiar with CARE, the nonprofit organization which supplies food, tools, and general aid all over the world, we lightly came to call our gifts CARE packages. Then one day I realized God had been sending me CARE packages all along—gifts to help me grow to be the kind of person he wanted me to be. Sometimes when they arrived I hadn't realized who had sent them, and sometimes they hadn't seemed to be anything I needed. And though

Preface

I may have greeted them with joy, after awhile many of them lay neglected on a shelf, gathering mold and mildew.

Why is there such a gap between what I am and what God wants me to be? I'm beginning to learn the answer to that dog-eared question. It's because I've neglected to use the gifts he gives me.

1.

The Gift of Self

If you could be any person in the world, who would you want to be? If it's someone other than yourself, you're your greatest enemy, because you are number one!

Uniqueness—the gift of self—is something God has bestowed on each of us. God made me to be an original, not a copy. My uniqueness comes from every thought, act, feeling, attitude, habit, and response which is totally me. Sure, I have traits in common with others, but there's something about me that's different from anyone who has ever lived.

My husband's counseling load as a minister would be cut in half if people could only learn to love themselves. Then they could love their neighbors. And if they could learn to be at peace with themselves, they'd be at peace with others—in the family, the church, and the world.

Someone once said that if you take away all the things you do—your roles, your titles, diplomas, income—what's left is what you are. And the extent to which you feel good about what's left is your self-image.

"It is a psychological truism," says John Powell in *The Secret of Staying in Love*, "that our attitudes toward others are conditioned by our fundamental attitudes toward ourselves. If I cannot openly and honestly acknowledge my own strengths and assets, I will not want anyone else to acknowledge his."[1] In other words, if I can't love myself, I don't want you to love yourself either. Yet the second greatest commandment is to love one's neighbor as oneself, and that's exactly what most of us do.

But isn't self-love bad? Not when we understand that self-love and selfishness are different. Erich Fromm insists in his book, *Escape from Freedom*, that they're the very opposite.[2] Selfish people, like greedy ones, fear they won't get enough; envy consumes them. They don't like themselves, much less anyone else.

Some years ago I realized I had tried to be so many things to so many people that I'd lost any sense of my own identity. All I had were roles I held or jobs I performed. I was my husband's helper, the minister's wife, the children's mother, my mother's daughter. I had been the president's secretary, the school's English and typing teacher, the doctor's bookkeeper, and so forth. But who was I really? I could exist no longer just as the reflection of someone else.

The search for the authentic self may be old hat to some of you, but until then, I'd never heard of anyone wanting to be his or her real self. I had spent some thirty-five years trying to be *somebody*, anyone other than the person I'd been all my life.

For me, the idea of looking for the real self had a certain backward sound to it—back to the grubby, hungry, share-

The Gift of Self

cropper days of postdepression whence I came. I didn't want to accept that self. For pete's sake, that was what I'd been trying to get away from all these years. It had never occurred to me that I might have real value just as I was. I didn't even want to sound like I was from Texas, and it has taken a great deal of effort to be able to write honestly about my search for my real self.

This book represents the thinking and research that grew out of my efforts to put order and purpose in my life, and to look at myself and evaluate what God has given me. It has taken me a long time to be able to accept what I found so that I could begin to grow as a person. And there's a lot I don't know yet. I've heard that Michelangelo said he sculptured his statue *David* by taking a block of granite and chipping away everything that wasn't David. I believe some of my growth came about that same way.

It would save time and agony if we could solve all of our problems by reading what someone else found out about himself or herself, but it's not that easy. So although I want to share some things that have helped me, remember that you have to do your own searching. I would encourage you, too, to listen to C. S. Lewis's suggestion that until you've given yourself to the Lord, you will not have a real self.

But you may say, "How can I love myself? I don't even know who I am." Our world is indeed filled with plastic faces. We wear so many masks that we don't know which one is real. And even as we begin to peel off these layers, at what point do we reach our authentic self?

The other day I heard of an eighty-year-old woman buying a tiny live oak tree to plant in her backyard. Knowing her grandmother's love for the big live oaks in the area, her granddaughter said, "Why, Granny, it'll take twenty or twenty-five years for that little sapling to grow big enough to shade your backyard." The old woman replied,

"Then run get the shovel, honey. We haven't a moment to lose."

And that's how I felt once I realized how many years I had wasted trying to be someone else. Here are some things I learned in my self-search:

You must dare to dig deep within yourself. Remember that only you know how to be you, and no one else can tell you how to find yourself. I believe you'll find something grand when you start looking.

There's an old story about an Indian chief who was carving a canoe out of a huge log. One of his braves came by and said, "Chief, I think she's too wide for her length." Later, another brave came by. "Chief, that stern's too full." A third brave advised, "The bow's way too sheer." And so the chief remodeled his canoe each time. Finally, the Indian finished the canoe and launched it in the river. It sank. He patiently hauled it up on the shore and cut down another tree. He'd hardly started on the new canoe when another brave wandered over to offer advice. The chief held up his hand to stop him and pointed to the monstrosity on the bank. "That boat over there, everybody's boat. This one, chief's boat."

Develop a tremendous desire to become. No direct object follows the word *become*. There's none to put there. Your whole life is a process of becoming: of growing, seeing, feeling, touching, and loving. You have fantastic potential once you get in touch with it.

This becoming process will never be finished. I can't find my authentic self and forget it. With every day, every new experience, and every relationship, I'm changing and becoming. The process is more of an unfolding, bit by bit, than an unveiling. I cannot say I've found *the* truth about who I am, but only that I've found *a* truth. I like Bob Dylan's words: "He who's not busy being born is busy dying."[3]

The Gift of Self

I will never be again as I was yesterday. If you knew me then, don't make the mistake of thinking that person is the same one you see today.

Finding the authentic self is hard work. It requires patience because it has taken us years to fashion the masks we wear. We are who we are because of heredity and environment. And mostly because of environment—the experiences of our lives, the people we've known, and their influence on us.

In one sense, we are who we are because of what people have told us. If your father had said you had no mechanical ability, you'd begin to think of yourself as one who couldn't fix things. Later when you behaved as your father described you, you might think of yourself as being authentic. And yet your true self may be quite different, buried under layers of other people's opinions, hopes, and dreams for you. Another person might violently react to his or her father's statement and become a mechanical engineer. Just to prove a point.

As I grow to know more about myself, I'm learning to like myself better. For example, I've always had the tendency to run myself down when others complimented me. If a guest praised the great dinner I cooked, I'd say, "Oh, it was nothing. The barbecue was too spicy, and the baked potatoes a little dry." It's been hard to learn to say, "Thank you. I tried to plan the menu and prepare the food so you'd enjoy it."

Conformity is a real hindrance in the search for self. The world teaches it, and our educational process seems geared to the principle of trying to make each one of us like everybody else. To a great extent, our ability to conform seems to govern our success.

I believe that education should be the process of helping us to discover our uniqueness and to teach us how to go on to develop that uniqueness. Then it must show us how to give it all away, because that's the only reason for having anything.

What would we be like today if all during our school years, our teachers and fellow students had said this to us: "How wonderful that you're so different. Show me your differences, and maybe I can learn from them"?

I dream of the day when we can approach students and say, "Find out what you want to know. Here are some tools to use. I'll help you. Go think, study, and dream. Go create." The word *motivation* would be phased out of education textbooks. People of all ages would learn and explore because they want to know. Because they must know.

Conformity invades the home too. Did you ever say to your son, "Eat your spinach, honey. Look at your big brother there. He's eating all of his." As parents, we teach our children to conform and then wonder why Johnny wants to do something just because "everybody's doing it."

I'm not saying parents and teachers should let kids grow up without any guidance and instruction. But we should help them to find their own uniqueness and then let them be just that.

According to a test conducted by the Foundation for Research on Human Behavior and published in *Creativity and Conformity* in 1958, women appear to conform more than men. That doesn't surprise me since, traditionally, society has expected women to fit into certain roles. But age is also important. These researchers found that college seniors, for example, conform less than college sophomores. And forty-year-old women conform less than female college seniors.[4]

When you hit a snag in your self-search, you might try some of these exercises.[5] I've found they're even more

The Gift of Self

helpful if you do them with a friend and share the results:

1. Draw a line graph of your life up to now, using a straight line to represent the "norm" and indicating the highs and lows in your life by points above and below the line. Show with an *x* the point at which you are right now. Remember that this is not your husband's or children's life, but *yours*. Try to draw some conclusions about yourself from the graph. Would you prefer to have drawn another kind of graph?

2. Write down on five separate pieces of paper at least five hats you wear—roles you perform in life. Use nouns, adjectives, verbs, or whatever. Then, put these pieces of paper in order of importance, placing on top the one you care least about. Look at each piece of paper and think about what your life would be without it. You might discover some new awareness of existence beyond these external dimensions.

3. Write a short paragraph of what you'd do on a typical day if you could be without any of the above roles. If necessary, go for a walk to loosen your imagination while you think. (If you can't bear to give up certain roles, that reveals something too.)

4. Now, what would you do on a very special day? With no cares, no responsibilities, and no limits? Pour in all the vanilla extract you want. Free yourself and dream away.

5. Dig back in your memory and write down the greatest experience you've ever had. Define it any way you wish. It can be the happiest, saddest, or the most momentous. Why did you choose that particular one?

6. List some things you do well and some things you'd like to do well.

7. List some things you do badly and/or would like to stop doing.

8. Think back to when you were growing up and write out answers to these questions: (Be honest!)
- What did you want from life then?
- What goals did you have for when you became an adult?
- Have you reached them?
- How did you feel about marriage? parenting? your sexuality?

If you could rewrite any of your answers above, what would they be? You may conclude, "I'm locked in by conforming to my parents in a foolish attempt to please." Or, "I'm rebelling against the past." So look into your heart again:
- What do you want from life now?
- What are your current personal goals?
- Do you think you'll reach those goals?
- How do you feel about marriage, parenting, and your sexuality now?

9. The following questions show how you rate yourself. On one end is the feeling of a tragic loser and the other a totally successful winner.
- How do you feel about yourself in general?

LOSER - WINNER

- How do you feel about what you've accomplished thus far in life?

LOSER - WINNER

- How do you feel about your relationships with others?

LOSER - WINNER

Are you satisfied with where you placed yourself on the scales above? What would you like to change? Take the

The Gift of Self

answers that dissatisfied you the most and begin working on them so you can feel like more of a winner.

10. Write a brief newsreel of your life several years off. If you prefer, think of it as an obituary. What do you want said about you?

These exercises are exciting to repeat at different stages in life. The results are different as you grow and become.

One happy serendipity has come my way in this search. I'm learning to be less critical and more accepting of others. Carl Rogers once said this: "When I accept myself as I am, I change, and when I accept others as they are, they change." The words of Henry David Thoreau have also taken on deeper meaning: "If a man does not keep pace with his companions, perhaps it is because he hears a different drummer. Let him step to the music he hears, however measured or far away."

I like what Rainer Maria Rilke says about searching for answers to life's questions: "Be patient toward all that is unsolved in your heart. And try to love the questions themselves. Do not seek the answers that cannot be given to you because you would not be able to live them. And the point is to live everything. Live the questions now. Perhaps you will then gradually, without noticing it, live along some distant day into the answer."[6]

God gave me the gift of myself, just as he gave you the gift of yourself. I'm the daughter of the King, just as you're his daughter or his son. We're neither superior nor inferior to anyone else, whether by sex, race, money, talent, or whatever. We're just different from each other, and we've got a lot of problems to work out. But remember what the popular saying tells us: "God don't make no junk."

Walt Whitman's "Song of Myself" was first published in 1855; the words are as new as anything written today. Its first three lines are particularly appropriate for us:

ALL THE THINGS YOU AREN'T . . . YET

I celebrate myself, and sing myself,
And what I assume you shall assume,
For every atom belonging to me as good belongs to you.

I believe that my ministry depends on my uniqueness.
God won't ask me why I wasn't Peter or Paul or Priscilla.
He'll ask me, "Why weren't you Jackie?"

2.

The Gift of the Mind

Ask almost any person to name the most intellectually stimulating person they know, and I'll bet it's not a woman! Which do you hear a group of women discuss most often? A challenging book they're reading, a new idea they've heard, their plans to improve a situation? Or latest fashions, complaints, and accomplishments of their children? To hear most women talk, it's indeed a drab world of dirty dishes, dirty diapers, and dirty rings-around-the-collar. "But that's all I see," you say? Yes, but you can do ionospheric thinking even while scrubbing the commode or mopping up grape-flavored Tang from the kitchen floor.

Women have traditionally been the most careless stewards of God's marvelous gift of the mind—women in general and Christian women in particular. If the progress in the world, in the church, or in any other situation had depended on our use of our intellect, we'd probably still be making clothes out of animal skins. Being a woman, I have found this to be very painful. We've often been content to blame others, circumstances, and bad luck when, as Shakespeare said in *Julius Caesar,* "The fault, dear Brutus, is not with our stars, but with ourselves. . . ."[1]

The Bible says a great deal about the mind and the intellect. From Proverbs 23:7 we learn we are literally what we think. We're the complete sum of all we think, and even our emotions flow from the thinking pattern of the mind. The emotional center of an individual is in the mind, and the condition of this center affects the condition of the entire body. A beautiful Godlike person isn't a thing of chance but a natural result of continued right thinking and long association with God. We will always be buffeted about by every little happening in our lives as long as we believe we're creatures of outside conditions. The circumstances of our lives don't make us what we are. They just reveal what we are to ourselves.

According to the *Random House Dictionary of the English Language,* the intellect is the power or faculty of the mind by which we know or understand, as distinguished from that by which we feel and that by which we will. Using this as the basis of our thinking in this chapter, let's first look at the seat of the intellect, the brain.

When you were two or three months old, your brain weighed less than one pound. Cells continued to form in your brain until you were one or two years old and continued to increase in size until you reached about fifteen years of age. An adult brain weighs about three pounds—just a good mess of green beans. Our intelligence doesn't depend on the weight of our brain. A genius may have a brain of only average weight while a less intelligent person may have a very heavy brain.[2]

The best estimates suggest that only a very few people

The Gift of the Mind

ever use more than 10 percent of their mental potential. Albert Einstein gave us the theory of relativity by which we were able to work out the basic problems of atomic energy. His intellectual powers were phenomenal, yet some experts estimate he used only about 2 percent of his mental capacity.

Why did God give us such intellectual capacity. Perhaps as a safety factor, for use in eternity, and to use now. What we do know is that our brain has enormous potential that is untapped. Joseph Conrad once said: "The mind of man is capable of anything because the human brain has everything in it."[3]

At one time I worked for Lockheed Electronics, one of the NASA contractors in Houston. The array of computers that our branch was concerned with occupied almost an entire floor of the office building. They could do everything but grill cheeseburgers. Yet that entire complex of computers couldn't do what my brain, or yours, can. According to the 1969 *World Book Encyclopedia*, it would take an electronic computer the size of the Empire State building to do the work of one human brain—if scientists could design one. Now that blows my mind.

And still more progress is being made every year. Just a few decades ago, according to writers Emily and Ola d'Aulaire, an entire electronic computer system that weighed thirty tons, filled warehouse-size rooms, and cost nearly $500,000, did what the basic pocket calculator does today. They attribute the heart of this success story to the tiny space-age "brain," which they describe as being "no bigger than a baby's fingernail, no more expensive than a gallon of milk. Each 'brain' consists of a crystal or 'chip,' of pure silicon, with the equivalent of thousands of transistors microscopically engraved on its mirrorlike surface." Peter Nelson of Hewlett-Packard, a major calculator manufacturer, says that if we'd stumbled upon such a pocket calculator just twenty years ago, "we'd have thought the chip came from Mars. There would have been no way to fathom its secrets." Today these pocket calculators are turned out by the millions, and many sell for less than $10.[4]

Mathematics, memorizing long poems, and studying the classical languages were once thought to improve the mind, but today more emphasis is placed on other methods that free the mind. An effective example used for many years in the business world and elsewhere is called brainstorming. This conference technique uses unrestrained and spontaneous participation for solving special problems, amassing information, or stimulating creative thinking. Alex F. Osborn claims that group brainstorming produces 70 percent more good ideas than an individual can.[5]

Whatever we put into our minds through our eyes or ears initiates response in our hearts and in turn motivates our bodies. If, however, the mind receives little input, the body responds in like manner.

In recent years I've discovered I have been a poor steward of God's gift of the mind. I haven't always been, but somewhere along the way my mind began to atrophy. I have observed that, in general, people seem more reluctant to develop their intellects than many of the other gifts. A number of reasons account for this attitude.

We have the attitude that God doesn't want us to think. Christians have often had reputations for being uneducated and nonintellectual. All too frequently, we are content to let our leaders do our thinking for us, a tendency that may represent a carry over from the Middle Ages. The church, the government, or even our own spouses cannot be responsible to God for the use of our gifts. We are.

Some feel the mind is one of the last frontiers, and the possibilities seem both wonderful and frightening. We can

The Gift of the Mind

idly speculate as to whether or not Adam and Eve wore goat skins or rabbit skins but questions concerning the One who created our minds require our deepest concentration. Living the Christian life and trying to understand God's will for us require all of our brainpower.

There's comfort in a closed mind. New ideas tend to frighten people—maybe because they make people unsure of themselves. William James once observed, "As a rule we disbelieve all facts and theories for which we have no use."

Why is it, when we think we've learned a new truth, we want to wrap it up into a neat package and set it on a shelf? We just quit looking. How comforting to have such vast knowledge! It's wonderful when we learn some of God's truth, but dangerous when we begin to think we know all of truth. There are new ideas around all the time, but all too seldom do we hear anyone say, "Tell me what you've learned. Maybe I can learn from you."

Remember too, we shouldn't just accept all new ideas, but test them out. Whatever is truth will stand up to all inquiries. It won't need protection.

When I was younger, I thought you climbed a mountain to reach a plateau. Now I realize you climb to climb. If you reach a spot where you can't see more rocks above you, you've probably fallen down the mountain. And whenever you get to the point where you see no more truths, you've fallen into an abyss. We have to continue to seek the truth, not because it's lost, but because we are.

Carl Ketcherside, a Christian writer and editor, once shared this thought in his writings, and it has become one of my favorite prayers. The original author is unknown to me.

> From the cowardice that shrinks from new truths,
> From the laziness that is content with half truths,
> From the arrogance that thinks it knows all truth.
> O God of all Truth, deliver us.

Reading is out of date. Even with our various means of communication, books are still our cheapest and handiest sources. The most intelligent people I know read as though they want to swallow whole bookcases in one gulp. They hunger for what other people say about their world.

Reading gets me out of my own time and place. It returns me to myself and helps define who I am. It places me in a relationship with human history and human effort. It locates me on the map of human experience and sets up points of reference whereby I can inspect myself. Reading gives me myself as material for thinking. And once I read a book, the people in it become a part of my own life.

Besides being a necessity, reading also serves as a luxury. A walk in the woods can't compare with a trip to Safeway. The first brings home a brightened face and lungs filled with good clean air. The second, a gallon of milk and a loaf of bread. I need both. I like what Elizabeth Alden Green said in *What to Read Before College:* "The reader who develops early the habit of exploring in all sorts of directions and looking for the unexpected should be rewarded his whole life by finding that his day-to-day experience and his changing interests extend his enjoyment of literature, which in turn enhances his pleasure in life."[6]

Is the person who won't read any better off than the one who can't? Dr. Robert Hutchins, former president of the University of Chicago, said: "We do not need to burn all the books to destroy our western civilization. All we need to do is leave them unread for one generation."

Don't tell me you haven't time to read. Shakespeare and whole-wheat bread recipes can be read side by side and even enhance your serving it for dinner. A sack lunch and a book or the Bible on a lunch hour at the office will help your pocketbook as well as your mind. And we both know that most people do just about what they really want to do. It's a matter of desire.

The Gift of the Mind

I like the way Aldous Huxley puts it: "Every man who knows how to read has it in his power to magnify, to multiply the ways in which he exists, to make his life full, significant and interesting."

Studying sounds so boring; I like to be where the action is. Whoever said that learning new ideas wasn't great fun? I often get a grim reaction from my students whenever I speak of using your intellect. I'm reminded of what was said about Frank O'Connor at a summer conference on the novel at Harvard. One of the invited speakers had given a rather portentous address on the responsibilities of the novelist. O'Connor, on the platform, had found himself giggling at each new solemnity. After the address, he walked to the lectern and said, "All right, if there are any of my students here I'd like them to remember that writing is fun."[7]

A challenging book or conversation can make an ordinary day exhilarating. In the classes I've taught over the years, I've often had other teachers ask me, "What was all that laughing I heard?" To their disturbed ears, it didn't sound like much learning was going on, but they were hearing the sound of people enjoying themselves, learning new ideas.

I read it once so I know what it says. Reading is often confused with thinking. They're related but not necessarily the same. There's a big difference in reading something and asking what it means. Study involves reading; then over a period of time, thinking about what you've read, comparing it to other knowledge, talking about it, doing research in other places, and always asking God's help in your understanding. Sometimes we do a little reading and think we've used our intellect.

Some of us have studied the Bible most of our lives, but we haven't the vaguest notion of what it says, much less how to apply it. As far as learning is concerned, adult

Bible classes can result in the most wasted hour in the week. Few classroom situations encourage the class members to be more than listeners. Without desks, notebooks and books must be balanced on our knees. When we become an audience of spectators, sitting in straight rows, looking at each other's backs, and waiting to be entertained, we deceive ourselves that we're students of the Word; we're merely students of the Bible School experience. A student is one who has a vocation for study.

Sharing sessions are popular these days, and they're great. But they shouldn't be confused with study sessions. Their purpose is different: to share what we've already learned, to seek mutual help and encouragement, or to celebrate a blessing in our lives.

There's a need to look not only at what an author says, but at what he whispers to us. It is amazing how many people can see or read of extraordinary events and come away with no change or growth inside. Author Pearl Buck has seen many crude happenings of nature in famine and flood, especially in China. "But," she once said, "there is nothing intrinsically interesting in such things except as they happen to some person. It is only what happens inside a person that is really drama and really exciting."[8]

Learning is for the young. You're as old as you think. There's a better recipe for staying young than the one for witch's brew in *Macbeth*, "the eye of a newt and the toe of a frog."[9] Using your intellect is one of the essential ingredients. I agree with artist Françoise Gilot, once married to Pablo Picasso, who said: "The reason creative people are never old is because each morning they are able to wonder, to ask questions like a child, and, maybe, find some new answers."[10]

It is commonly thought that a man's ability to function, physically or mentally, automatically plummets at age sixty-five or seventy. Not so, says Dr. Alexander Leaf, a physician

The Gift of the Mind

and teacher of doctors, who has made a study of three regions where people live longest.[11] Compared to young people, elderly people score higher on vocabulary tests but are slower in responding mentally. This happens because they consider more information than young people do, according to research by Dr. James E. Birren, Director of U.S.C.'s Gerontology Center.[12] And in his opinion, many changes observed in the middle-aged brain are simply phenomena of disuse.[13]

There are even some advantages, says choreographer George Balanchine: "Old people don't get tired—it's only the young who tire. Confusion exhausts them. I've got more energy now than when I was younger because I know exactly what I want to do."

Parents often ask, "How can we teach our children to use their intellect?" Just don't stifle them, I would advise. They're born with curiosity. Remember when they first began to talk? "Why do dogs bark? Bullfrogs croak? Where does light come from? How come we need to keep clean?" So you don't know the answers? Look them up. Sometimes children ask questions and aren't able to understand the answers, but don't squelch them. We can teach our children everything we know, and that won't necessarily amount to much. But if we can teach them to learn by encouraging their curiosity, they'll continue the learning process as long as they live.

We need to create an air of openness and curiosity; we need to challenge them to think. I consider it a good conversation with my sons when more questions are raised than answers given. And as a schoolteacher, I've contended that a real classroom is not where we come to have all our questions answered, but where we're challenged to find our own answers. This is the hardest kind of teaching for either parents or teachers.

And then, having provided this kind of environment, we have to stand back and let our children do as we've encouraged them—let them think for themselves.

Even when a person wants to use God's gift of the mind, one runs into many problems:

Peer group pressure to conform. It's more comforting to do as others do. Few people respect your saying, "I can't stay for lunch. I'm reading a book this afternoon." Worse than that is, "I'm going for a walk in the country." In some cities where we've lived, I've become a professional college student just to have a legitimate excuse for using my mind.

Good causes. The Band Parents club, the PTA, and the Cancer Drive are all worthwhile. Indeed, there's no end to the number of good causes. Too often, we don't choose them, they choose us. We have twenty-four hours like everyone else. We have to decide how we'll spend them or others will decide for us.

Illness. Good health is one of God's great blessings. But hundreds of invalids attest that almost any illness can be dealt with—if the desire is strong enough.

Fatigue. No one can will oneself to think if one's body is always tired. The reasons are many: overwork, poor diet, and lack of exercise. Or because one's recreation doesn't re-create.

Apathy and lethargy. These are probably the greatest hazards of all. Edison defined genius as 1 percent inspiration and 99 percent perspiration.

"But my work takes up my whole day," you say. Or, "My husband could win the Barefoot & Pregnant Award from NOW (the National Organization for Women)." That husband might be interested to know that Manfred F. De-Martino, psychology professor at Onondaga Community College, says highly intelligent women are sexier than women of average intelligence. It's all there in his book, *Sex and the Intelligent Woman*.[14]

Lack of exercise. Much research has proved that brain cells deprived of sufficient oxygen do not perform their work efficiently, and intellect and reasoning powers fade as a result. Dr. Herbert A. de Vries, of the University of Southern California, came to the conclusion after he'd conducted some tests with retired men in their fifties and older, that exercise not only increased their physical stamina, slimmed down waistlines, and improved blood-pressure readings; the most striking result was the improvement in their "oxygen-transport capacity"—the amount of oxygen each heartbeat delivers to the rest of the body. This was demonstrated in some tests at Veterans Administration Hospital in Buffalo, New York, when clinical psychologists administered pure oxygen to senile patients placed in a pressurized chamber. After fifteen days, the patients' scores on standard memory tests jumped as much as 25 percent.[15]

Lack of good eating habits in general. The brain is affected by the fuel we feed our body. The controversy over use of refined sugars, white flour, and additives waxes hot. More and more people are becoming aware of the hazards of the American diet in general. It's worth checking into if you aren't feeling on top of the world, or if you just hope to stay that way. It boils down to this: What is good health worth to you?

I don't mean to imply that every moment should be spent improving your intelligence. I firmly believe in daydreaming, in sitting in the sun and watching the snails whizz by. At certain times the mind should be open, empty, and placid. But we can avoid intellectual curvature of the spine, which results from lounging on the back of our mental neck.

Learning is the only thing that never fails us even when

we "grow old and trembling in our anatomies" and "lie awake at night listening to the disorders of our veins," as English novelist Terence H. White once said. Learning can never be exhausted; it is unending. A mind that insists on knowing *must* learn just as a dog must eat.

When we stretch our minds to a new idea, they never go back to their original dimension. Neither do we.

There's a story about a small child who, day after day, watched a sculptor working on a marble slab. At last there came the moment when the child caught her breath in amazement and said to the sculptor, "But how did you know there was a lion in there?" There are lions in our minds just like that. But they can't be brought out without a lot of thinking.

3.

The Gift of Abilities

By definition, subversive *is the tendency to overthrow existing* structure. And so I warn you at the beginning that the purpose of this chapter is subversive, for we need something to jolt us out of our usual way of thinking.

Whenever I speak of God's gift of abilities, I often hear comments like these:

"I never had the opportunity to look inside and determine what my abilities were. I had to do the work before me. And it had to be the one that paid the most money."

"Are you joking? I've got four kids. My work chose me; I never chose it."

"I think I was born knowing I wanted to be a mother (or teacher or whatever). It's all I ever wanted to be so I never even looked into other areas."

"Can you believe I'm fifty years old and still don't know what God wants me to do with my talents?"

Booker T. Washington wrote in his autobiography, *Up from Slavery*, that he believed a Negro boy actually had advantages. Sure he had to work harder, but out of the struggle, he gained a strength and confidence that he missed when life was smooth. He went on to say: "I have learned that success is to be measured not so much by the position that one has reached in life as by the obstacles which he has overcome while trying to succeed."[1]

Many people stumble through life half-heartedly, doing a little of this and a piddling of that. They feel hemmed in by the demands of those around them. They imagine the world is against them, and they subconsciously conspire to make it true. Considering it a waste of time to experiment with new abilities, they demonstrate that the impossible is usually the untried. Hung up on high center, they never raise their sights beyond pleas of "Lord, bless this mess."

Talent is the skill or ability or power to perform. It's whatever you are able to do. The word *talent* is a Middle English word from the Greek word *talanton*, which referred to a balance or weight or monetary unit. The familiar parable of the talents in Matthew 25 refers specifically to three men who were given different amounts of money according to their ability. The first two men doubled their amount, but the third hid his. Is it fair that his only talent was then taken from him and given to the one who had the most?

The parable of the pounds in Luke 19 is a similar one. These three men all had the same amount, but they differed in the amount they gained. The third man hid his, and so his one pound was taken away and given to the one who had the most. Fair or not, Jesus said that's the way it's done. The one who did the most with his gift was given the most. And let me clearly say, I believe Jesus' lesson is directed to all of us, male or female.

The Gift of Abilities

Both of these parables are not concerned specifically with the gift of money nor the gift of talents or degrees of reward. But the talents or pounds represent any gifts God has given to us. As with all our gifts, we run the risk of losing them if we don't use them or if their potential is lost. Not only that, it's an insult to God, the giver.

Many women in particular are troubled these days about God's purpose for them. Following the "big yellow road" hasn't always led to happiness. But I think women have often been psyched out when they confront this task of uncovering their talents. After all, doesn't everyone know what talents a Christian woman is supposed to have? You know, baking bread, tending the sick, teaching children, and so forth.

Emerson must have been looking into the future to today's women when he said: "Our chief want in life is someone who can make us do what we can."[2]

We all know there's a big difference between having something to do and having to do something. Being a wife and being a mother are wonderful. They require as many of our talents as do being a good husband and father. But what about the rest of our talents? I know all these demands on us aren't meant to tear us apart but to add new dimension to our lives. We don't want to have an affair with our alibis, but we don't want to be cowards either. What about these dreams we've had? Surely God didn't give them to us just to pass the torch of our dreams on to our children? They'll have their own dreams in life.

The problem with this gift is not one of definition. Many of us have moved from the point of thinking we're no-talent people to knowing that we have many talents. The feeling we have is similar to what Mark Twain must have felt about spring fever: ". . . You don't quite know what it is you want, but it just fairly makes your heart ache, you want it so."

Sometimes I seem to have questions no one else is asking, but I agree with James Thurber that it's better to ask some of the questions than to know all the answers.

What difference does it make if I use my abilities or not? When Jesus told the young ruler in Matthew 19 to sell what he had and give to the poor, Jesus wasn't interested in the money. He was interested in the young man. When God gives me gifts, he's asking me to be the caretaker of them; mainly, because of what it will do for me.

How much ability do I really want? People naturally expect more of a ten-talent person than a two-talent one. The more I do, the more I'll be asked to do. But the more I do, the more I'll be able to do. And the more I do, the more it will mean to me. We often only want to admit we're ten-talent sinners.

We tend to think we have fewer abilities than we actually have. We may say, "I'm sure I don't have the talent to be a pilot or an engineer or whatever." But how do we know? One of the delights in being adventurous is discovering new things about ourselves. And nothing would be done at all if we waited until we could do it so well no one could find fault with it. Arthur Koestler wrote in *The Act of Creation* that "the more original a discovery, the more obvious it seems afterwards."[3]

Our problem is not in greatness or smallness of abilities but in our motivation to use them. We don't find our talents by hunting for them so much as expanding the ones we're already aware we have. We expand our talents as we expand our use of them, and each new effort adds something to our world and to ourselves. The process is like turning on the lights. The house won't be fully lighted until the last switch is thrown.

Do we have different abilities now because we were born with them or because we've used them differently? God gave us something to begin with, but we've had different experiences

The Gift of Abilities

and opportunities. Aldous Huxley observed, "Experience is not what happens to a man. It is what a man does with what happens to him." I would add, "everyday." It was Kafka, I believe, who said he could not understand why some people were so disdainful of everyday life since that was the only one they had. And maybe the crush of people around us affects us. Goethe thought that talent was produced in solitude while character was formed in the stream of life.

The way we take advantage of opportunities has something to do with developing our abilities too. So often we overlook opportunities right before us because we're so nearsighted we fail to detect their presence.

Making the rounds a few years back was this story of a guard at a construction plant. He stopped a man who was pushing a wheelbarrow of straw out through the gates. The guard searched the wheelbarrow and sifted through the straw but found nothing.

"Something's not right here," the guard told the man. "But I can't figure out what you're doing. Go on through."

The next day the same man appeared at the gate with another wheelbarrow full of straw. Again the guard went over every inch of the wheelbarrow and sifted through the straw. Again he found nothing and was forced to let the man go through.

On the third occasion, however, the guard's suspicions forced him to take the man to his chief for questioning.

"We know you're stealing something," the chief said. "Tell you what. We'll make a gentleman's agreement with you. You tell us what you're taking, and we won't press charges, provided you stop it."

So the man confessed: "What I've been stealing is wheelbarrows."

Do you have an ability no one else has? A specific job that only you can do? You might do with pleasure what thou-

sands could do and leave undone what was only meant for you. Martin Buber said, "Every single man is a new thing in the world and is called upon to fulfill his particularity in this world. Who knows but what you have come into the world for such a time as this?"[4]

Someone has said we all start out originals and tend to end up copies. But I wonder if we start out fairly identical copies and end up originals, because of the use of our gifts.

Just because you've tried and failed doesn't mean you can't do it. When a door slams before you, look for the one God is opening.

In one of my favorite *Peanuts* cartoons, Charlie Brown says, "When you've lost at something, you can react in two ways . . . one way is to analyze just how you lost . . . try to figure out what your weaknesses were, and then try to improve so that next time you can win . . ." Snoopy, lying on his back on top of his doghouse, says, "Bleah!" And Charlie shrugs and says, "That's the other way."

"I know it can be done," an old New England ship carpenter said about a difficult job of construction. But when asked how he knew, he said, "Don't ask me so many questions. I can't understand all I know."

It may be that your limits have bordered on the true edge of necessity—that which you've been pushed into doing, that which was absolutely necessary. Barring certain physical and mental limitations, with God's help you can do anything you want to do. And he's certainly willing for you to expand your abilities tenfold and more. The number of abilities you have today is the number you've wanted it to be—because of the belief you have in yourself and in the Lord.

Sometimes we say we'd like to have greater ability, but we aren't willing to pay the price. A young voice student

The Gift of Abilities

came to hear a very talented singer one night and sat on the front row in the concert hall. He listened with awe at the beautiful voice and skill of the artist. When he was finished, the young student said, "Oh, that was wonderful. Why, I'd give anything to be able to sing like that. Why, I'd give a . . . a dollar!" And so we would. What we'd like to be differs considerably from what we're willing to sacrifice to become whatever we'd like to be.

Our abilities may never reach our hopes, but we must be confident enough and humble enough to think they can. "Always think of what you have to do as easy," Emile Coué, a French psychotherapist, is reported to have said, "and it will become so."

Is it better to be a jack-of-all-trades or develop a few abilities to a high degree? That depends on you. Personally, I am fragmented when I spread myself too thin. There's a wonderful story in education circles that Dr. Leo Buscaglia, of the University of Southern California, once told a conference of the Texas Association for Children with Learning Disabilities. It's about the Animal School. It seems that some animals got together and decided to start a school. They formed a Board of Education with a rabbit, a bird, a squirrel, a fish, and an eel. When they wrote a curriculum guide for their school, the rabbit insisted that they include running. The bird voted for flying, the fish for swimming, and the squirrel insisted on tree-climbing. Then they all insisted all animals take all of the subjects. The rabbit was making A in running, but he kept falling on his head in tree-climbing until he couldn't even run very well. Pretty soon he was making C in running and of course an F in tree-climbing. The bird was terrific at flying, but he kept breaking his wings in other courses and shortly was making C in flying and F in everything else. The moral of the story is that the valedictorian of the class turned out to be a mentally retarded eel. But everyone was happy because they were all taking all of the subjects. We call this ridiculous, yet we continue on the path of trying to be like everyone else and committing suicide.

To help pinpoint where you are in your own abilities, draw or paint some sort of picture that shows how you feel about your use of God's gift of abilities. Or, if you could drink a magic potion that would solve all your problems concerning abilities, what would it be?

As you consider this, don't underestimate the importance of your ability, no matter how small it seems to you. I remember what one of the secretaries at NASA told me one day when I was admiring some pictures of the moon walk hanging on her office wall.

"It must have been exciting to work here when this was happening," I said to her.

"Well, we all did our part," she answered as she looked up from the bimonthly report she was typing. "The astronauts never would have even made it to the moon without everyone else. And Liquid Paper," she added as she made a typing correction.

I've never been able to trace the author of this sensitive poem:

> "Master, where shall I work today?"
> And my love flowed warm and free;
> And he pointed out a tiny plot,
> And said, "Tend that for Me."
>
> But I answered quickly, "Oh no, not there;
> Not anyone could see
> No matter how well my task was done . . .
> Not that little place for me."
>
> And His voice, when He spoke, it was not stern,
> But he answered me tenderly:

The Gift of Abilities

> "Disciple, search that heart of thine;
> Are you working for them, or for Me?
> Nazareth was just a little place,
> And so was Galilee."

Using your talents is a *now* concept. God doesn't want you feeling guilty for the way you've messed up your talents in the past. What He does want is to free you and focus your energies on the use of your abilities today. Go forth with confidence. Then you'll begin to see your own unique purpose in life.

I've worn several different hats during my life—secretary, wife, mother, accountant, business woman, homemaker, teacher, and free-lance writer. At times my sons have asked, "Say, Mom, what are you gonna be when you grow up?" I can see the steps I've gone through in gaining each new ability, even in the writing of this book. And I can somewhat identify with Sarasate, the great Spanish violinist of the last century, who was once called a genius by a famous critic. In reply to this, Sarasate shook his head and snorted: "Genius! For thirty-seven years I've practiced fourteen hours a day, and now they call me a genius."

My abilities have changed over the years and will continue to change as I open up myself to new experiences. Change is the most striking characteristic of the world we live in, and it's evident of growth. Change has always been a part of life.

The crucifixion and death of Jesus was terrible but necessary for his body to change into a glorified body. We see the grass wither and die only to spring to life again. Man is born and dies and goes back to dust. But in all of it, God is at work, for he is Lord of change. His unchanging nature itself makes change possible, and he brings things into being and allows them to change and pass away. Yet,

ALL THE THINGS YOU AREN'T . . . YET

at the same time he remains our stability in a transient world.

There's no end to the questions and answers to "What can I do?" I could tell you how I use my talents, but what you want to know is how to find and expand ways to use your gifts. Albert Einstein insisted that imagination was more important than knowledge.

The following are some of the questions that have helped me. Try writing down the answers and then sharing the results with a group of friends. "Look with your understanding, find out what you already know, and you'll see the way to fly," Jonathan Livingston Seagull would remind us.

1. How long have you been actively searching for your abilities?
2. What are your talents and abilities today? List each one.
3. How do you know you have these abilities?
4. Which is your very best ability? Why is it your best?
5. Where did you get these abilities? Probe way back.
6. What possible abilities do you think you have but have never developed?
7. What are some abilities you definitely do not have? How do you know?
8. What abilities are you presently working on expanding?
9. What is the most wonderful ability you can think of possessing? Why is it so important?
10. Do you at least have a little of that wonderful gift? What are you doing about it?
11. Do you know the absolute limit of your abilities?
12. How often do you pray about your gift of abilities?
13. In what way is the use of your abilities helping you? Consider the use of each ability individually.

The Gift of Abilities

Over my desk I have a bulletin board on which I tack up quotes and ideas. These words from Henry David Thoreau have looked down on me daily for over ten years: "I learned this, at least, by my experiment: that if one advances confidently in the direction of his dreams, and endeavors to live the life which he has imagined, he will meet with a success unexpected in common hours. . . . If you have built castles in the air, your work need not be lost; that is where they should be. Now put the foundations under them."

All of us need someone to believe in us, but more than that, we all need to believe in ourselves. Goethe said: "What you can do, or dream you can, begin it: Boldness has genius, power and magic in it."

All of us are walled in by circumstances, but we have to push out against the walls to be sure where they are. If we don't push the walls out, they'll push us in. Most of us have less freedom to develop our talents than we'd like but more freedom than we think we have.

Let's not settle for the abilities we now have. Let's be willing to sacrifice what we are for what we can become. George Bernard Shaw once said it like this: "Be sure to get what you like or else you will have to like what you get."

4.

The Gift of the Body

Paul urges in Romans 12:1: ". . . present your bodies a living and holy sacrifice, acceptable to God. . . ." He reminds us again in 1 Corinthians 6:13 that "the body is for the Lord and the Lord is for the body" and asks in verses 19 and 20: "Or do you not know that your body is a temple of the Holy Spirit who is in you, whom you have from God, and that you are not your own? For you have been bought with a price: therefore glorify God in your body."

According to W. E. Vine's *Expository Dictionary of New Testament Words,* the Greek word used here for "temple" is *naos,* meaning a shrine or sanctuary, a structure set apart to God.[1]

I think a healthy, well-cared-for body has to be included in the many wonderful ways we glorify God. But it's only the beginning point, to be sure. Yet most of us continue to misuse and desecrate this holy gift, of which God himself said after he had made it, that it was very good.

Care of the body makes sense even to people who aren't concerned with the Spirit of God living within them—not just so it will last longer, for there's no particular merit in living longer if you're miserable in the process, but to enjoy a better quality of life in the meantime.

Care of the body is not an end in itself, but good physical health makes for good mental health, which contributes to good spiritual health, and so on. The misuse of any in this triad brings on suffering in the other two areas.

Some two hundred thousand people a year go to the famed Mayo Clinic with every malady known to medical science. What they really want to know is, "How can I feel better and live longer?" Yet many could have prevented the illness for which they come. Dr. Bruce E. Douglass, chairman of the division of environmental medicine at Mayo, says, "To a greater extent than ever before, barring accidents, longevity is up to the individual." [2]

The general public is endlessly intrigued with affairs of health. In looking over the hundreds of articles and books written on the body, most of the advice of experts falls into these categories:

Cultivate good health. Feeling plain lousy seems to be a way of life in America. Infectious diseases such as the plague and tuberculosis used to be a major cause of lowered average life expectancies. Today's human being is often tortured by degenerative diseases, and more and more a prime offender seems to be the food we eat. Candy bars, soft drinks, and empty calories aren't wholly to be blamed, but the culprit is the basic food we eat every day, the staple diet. Kicking the sugar habit is becoming a matter of great concern, alongside kicking the smoking habit. One doctor posted on his office door a sign which read,

"The doctor is on vacation. Cut down on everything and come back next month."

Health food stores have continued to multiply over the nation. And countless books on the subject of good nutrition are on every book rack. In recent years information has been published on adding food fiber or roughage to your diet. Dr. David Reuben, in his popular book *The Save-Your-Life Diet,* says that a high-roughage reducing diet will not only regulate proper bowel activity, reduce the likelihood of developing heart disease, diabetes, and high blood pressure, but will enable you to lose excess weight gradually and safely. And of all the threats to our health, obesity is potentially one of the most lethal. Like charity, obesity begins in your own home, usually in the kitchen. With the proper diet, your weight will slowly come down to the ideal level and stay there. An added benefit is that a high-roughage diet seems to induce tranquility, and most people even find it easier to fall asleep at night. Dr. Reuben claims that the pleasure of feeling satisfied, knowing that your body is finally functioning as it should—and losing weight in the process—may make it impossible ever to go back to your old ways of eating.[3] And more and more people, including my own family, can personally attest to that fact.

Men can add eleven years to their lives if they follow seven golden rules of behavior, according to a study conducted since 1965 on residents of Alameda County by a team of California researchers. Women can add seven years to their lives the same way. The golden rules are: eating regularly and not between meals; eating breakfast; getting eight hours of sleep a night; keeping a normal weight (being neither overweight nor underweight); not smoking; drinking moderately (no more than one or two alcoholic beverages a day); and exercising regularly.

"A man at age fifty-five who follows all seven good health

habits has the same physical health status as a person twenty-five to thirty years younger who follows less than two of the health practices," said Dr. Lester Breslow, dean of the school of public health at the University of California at Los Angeles and an author of the same study.[4]

Federal health experts agree that the daily health habits of clean living have more to do with what makes people sick and when people die than all the preventive and health care services combined, even with all the advances in surgery, antibiotics, and anesthesia. The eleven-year increase in longevity is especially striking, said Breslow, since from 1900 to 1970 the life expectancy of American men increased by only three years and for American women, seven years.

Dr. Bruce E. Douglass said that most patients come to the Mayo Clinic with the dangerous misconception that it's normal to gain weight as they grow older. If at thirty you weigh 170 pounds and keep the same weight at sixty, you may still be carrying a hazardous excess. "Fat people usually don't grow old," Dr. Douglass said.[5]

Be optimistic. Optimism can make you beautiful, the behavior experts say. The smile on your face may not make you look like Raquel Welch, but it'll do a lot for your state of health. According to a newspaper interview with Douglas Radabaugh, assistant professor in social work at the University of Houston, "There is no doubt that an optimistic state of mind keeps the body running in top shape."[6]

On the other hand, pessimism is more likely to lead to depression, which actually slows down all of your metabolic functions and increases your susceptibility to illness. Radabaugh suggests, if you feel a depressive mood coming on, that you take some form of action, even if it's only making a mental decision. Physical exercise is also recommended.

A personal friend, Dale Graham, Minister of Pastoral Care for a church in Pasadena, Texas, concurs that it's extremely therapeutic for a severely depressed person to be able to do something. He usually suggests something specific for him or her to do in the next thirty minutes or before going to bed that night. Getting the depressed person to do anything is important, whether it's one who is mildly depressed or one who is threatening suicide. Action clears away the cobwebs. An even more helpful assignment is to get the person to do something for someone else.

Physiologically, happiness is health. "A joyful heart is good medicine," says Proverbs 17:22, "but a broken spirit dries up the bones." Doctors repeatedly emphasize that a person can will himself to be ill, and the illness will be just as real as that of a person who is physically diseased.

Happiness and health generally go together. Happy people tend to be ill less often and recover more quickly. Their bones and tissues even seem to heal better. And happy people appear to age more slowly, besides having better color, glossier skins, and more erect carriages.

Watch your emotional stress. "A motor car doesn't suddenly cease running because of old age. It stops because of the failure of some part that has worn out. It's the same way with people under continuous stress, either physical or mental. Some vital body part gives way, leading to a variety of illnesses and eventually to death." This explanation comes to us from Dr. Hans Selye, director of the University of Montreal's Institute of Experimental Medicine & Surgery, in a *Today's Health* interview with J. D. Ratcliff.[7]

The word *stress* is borrowed from physics and engineering, Dr. Aaron T. Beck, professor of psychiatry at the University of Pennsylvania Medical School, points out in an interview in *U.S. News and World Report.* He defines stress as a force of sufficient magnitude to distort or deform when applied to a system. The two major types of stress are: the stress involved in loss—of a loved one, a job, or of self-esteem; and the stress involved in threats—to status, goals, health, security. These bring on symptoms of depression or anxiety and may involve 20 percent of Americans at one point or another in their lives.

Dr. Beck agrees with most experts who say we need to give our children opportunity to confront various problems when they're young so they can learn to cope. Intervention by parents deprives them of developing tolerance for problems and acquiring problem-solving mechanisms.

There's a limit to the amount of stress brought on by change that a human can take. The *U.S. News and World Report* article shares a scale devised by Dr. Thomas H. Holmes, professor of psychiatry at the University of Washington. This chart assigns point values to changes, good and bad, that often affect us. For example, he rates the death of a spouse at 100 points, divorce at 73, getting married at 50. Pregnancy rates 40, a change to a different job 36, change in residence as 20, and vacations as 13. When enough changes occur during one year to add up to 300, 80 percent of the people become seriously depressed or suffer other serious illness.[8]

Alvin Toffler coined the term *future shock* to describe "the shattering stress and disorientation that we induce in individuals by subjecting them to too much change in too short a time." His best seller, *Future Shock*, tells what happens to people when they are overwhelmed by change and looks at the ways in which we adapt—or fail to adapt—to the future.[9]

Not all stress is bad. Some stress is the salt of life; it wakes us up and makes us live. But difficulties arise when a particular stress, either mental or physical, is applied for too long. In his interview with *Today's Health*, Dr. Selye pointed out that the worst stresses are hatred, frustration, and anxiety. Experiments have been made in anxiety by placing a mouse and a cat in adjoining cages. The result for the mouse: he dies.

It's not the hated person who gets the ulcers, hypertension, and heart problems. It's the one who hates. "Love thy neighbor" continues to be one of the sagest bits of medical advice ever given. Whatever you do, one rule should be observed: don't go to bed in a state of emotional turmoil. Exercise is often much better.

Boredom and monotony, continuous exposure to loud noises, jammed subways or lunch counters, and family arguments are all potential stress areas. No matter what the nature of the stress, the same type of internal wreckage results. The question to ask is, "Is it worth it?"

To help combat stress, many Christians have learned the value of periods of quiet meditation. Even those who consider themselves nonreligious seek ways to satisfy their longing for inner tranquility and ways to cope with stress. They look to Transcendental Meditation, est (Erhard Seminar Training), encounter groups, a plan for biorhythms or how to control the brain's alpha waves. Some try Yoga, don saffron robes, and chant segments of "Hare Krishna."

Virtually everyone is struck by emotionally induced illness at some time. Dr. John A. Schindler, author of *How to Live 365 Days a Year,* insists, "Over 50 percent of all the illness that doctors see is emotionally-induced illness."[10] Other doctors estimate it varies from 60 to nearly 100 percent. Schindler also points out that the surprising thing is that these are people who don't have a great amount of trouble. The majority actually have very little real trouble, he says, but they've never learned to maintain good healthy emotions in just plain everyday living. They go mountain-climbing over molehills. They've never learned how to meet ordinary life situations with emotions like courage, cheerfulness, and determination, instead of anxiety, fear, and frustration. He points out that it's often easier to be calm in the face of great tragedy than it is to be poised and quiet in the face of life's little irritations, the sand-in-the-shoes type that overwhelms the person who lacks emotional maturity.

A friend sent me a clipping in which William C. Menninger, of the Menninger Foundation in Topeka, named these characteristics of emotional maturity:

1. Having the ability to deal constructively with reality.
2. Having the capacity to adapt to change.
3. Having a relative freedom from symptoms that are produced by tensions and anxieties.
4. Having the capacity to find more satisfaction in giving than receiving.
5. Having the capacity to relate to other people in a consistent manner with mutual satisfaction and helpfulness.
6. Having the capacity to sublimate, to direct one's instinctive hostile energy into creative and constructive outlets.
7. Having the capacity to love.

Don't worry. Someone once said worry was like a rocking chair; it gives you something to do but won't get you anywhere. Others defend worry on the basis that it's proof of care and concern. You can call it vertical or constructive worrying, but when it devours your energy, undermines your health, and renders life miserable, it will still shorten your life. There's a thin line between concern and worry, but it's there.

When the Lord told us not to be anxious for our lives, as to what we will eat or drink or for our bodies, he was not stressing irresponsibility about these matters. He was emphasizing that these things come from God, who knows what we need even before we ask. We want a healthy concern over the big things, but we need a kind of "roll-with-the-punch" attitude over little things. The slight difference between concern and worry appears when we begin to think it's all up to us and forget to rely on God. We need to let God do the worrying. We can get peptic ulcers from it; he can't!

What do we worry about anyhow? On occasions when you are vaguely disturbed, try making a list of what's bothering you. If you're like most people, your list will be vague and indefinite. Experts say that, of the things most people worry over, 40 percent never happen; 30 percent concern things over and past that can't be changed; 12 percent, needless health worries; and 10 percent, petty, miscellaneous worries. That leaves a legitimate 8 percent to worry over. In effect, what we dread, in reality rarely happens.

There's often less danger in the things we fear than in the things we desire. Thus financial worries rank high on everyone's list. The solution is in cutting down on our wants and simplifying our life. We may find, as Thoreau did, how many things we can do without.

Worrying about something before it happens is too early. Worrying about it afterwards is too late. What we need is to redirect this energy into more productive channels.

I think one of the shortest courses in "How to Keep from Worrying" must be the advice given in Charlie Schulz's *Peanuts*. Franklin, sitting at a desk at school, says, "I'll never get this second problem!" Peppermint Patty whispers, "Just put down 'eleven,' Franklin, and don't worry about it . . . that's what I did. 'X' is almost always eleven, and 'Y' is almost always nine. One thing I've learned about Algebra . . . don't take it too seriously. . . ."

Watch your energy level. Energy is the name given to the ability to do work. All human life depends upon energy, most of which comes from the sun. The cycle goes like this: The sun gives off rays which travel to the earth. Plants use it to make food which gives energy to men and animals. The sun's energy is also stored up in fuels like coal, wood, and oil which we burn to do work for us. Evaporated from the earth by the sun, water falls to earth again as rain. Rivers then flow and produce other useful energy. In fact, the history of man's development has often been described as the history of the discovery of new sources of energy to use for work.

I've known people in wheelchairs who seem to have a great deal of vitality, and others in seemingly good health who were listless. Some people just seem to feel like the morning after the night before, and "they ain't been anywhere." And then others of us take our energy for granted and squander it until one day it's gone.

"I'm always so tired" is a common complaint in every doctor's office. So much so that one doctor commented that most of his patients seem to suffer from year-round spring fever.

According to the *World Book Encyclopedia*, "The law of conservation of energy states that the amount of energy in the universe is always the same. It can neither be increased or lessened." The encyclopedia further explains that "it may be developed from matter and turned into matter." Technically, you can get only as much energy out of any machine as you put into it, but much of the useful energy is wasted by friction in the form of heat. This friction eventually causes a machine to run down.

With this in mind, let's look at some ways to cut down on the energy waste in our lives by reducing the friction:[11]

1. Plan your work ahead of time. Continually trying to decide what to do wastes your energy. Doctors say we have monthly, and even daily cycles of energy. And some have more energy in the morning while others have more in the afternoon. Whatever your peak period is, do the

most difficult jobs then and save your routine work for the lull.

2. Enlist the aid of your family. Help them to understand that efficiency is just intelligent laziness. It's important to give children plenty of freedom in their own room, but other parts of the home can be kept straight. Encourage them to put things back where they belong.

3. Arrange your materials to save energy. If you find yourself regularly walking from one place to another, there may be a way to limit those steps. Your work areas need to be reviewed occasionally to select the best places for putting the equipment you use most often.

4. Decide on a major and minor. Not even the most efficient person has time and energy to be an expert in every area. Select an activity you excel in and enjoy, and feel free to spend more energy there. If you major in cooking, look for the easiest ways to wash and clean. One man I know who works all day as an engineer looks for simple ways to keep the yard work to a minimum so he can enjoy flying radio-controlled model airplanes with his son. And keep in mind the energy which will be required to clean and maintain any new purchases you make for your family or the home.

5. Don't waste your energy. Just as friction wears down a machine, certain things spend your own energy. Wasted motion and indecision and outbursts of emotion such as anger, worry and fear drain your emotions. I like what British author Katherine Mansfield once suggested: "Make it a rule never to regret and never to look back. Regret is an appalling waste of energy; you can't build on it; it's only good for wallowing in."[12]

Conservation of energy is very much in the news these days. Energy experts tell us to put in more insulation, adjust the thermostat, and avoid fast take-offs that burn up excessive gas in our automobile. We need to look for similar ways to do this in the care of the physical body.

For example, if you're always beat at the end of the day, try pacing yourself more carefully. Maybe you're trying to do too much. Lying down for a few minutes or taking a hot bath sometimes helps. Nervous fatigue in some people can be caused by insufficient exercise. Take up jogging, tennis, or at least go for long walks in the fresh air. If you're tired from boredom, maybe you need a new job, a new hobby, some new friends, some new books, or at least a change of scenery.

6. Eat plenty of all kinds of energy-building foods that have thiamin, riboflavin, and niacin in them. Potassium, magnesium, and aspartic acid have been claimed by some doctors to be beneficial in relieving physical and emotional fatigue. Both magnesium and potassium play an important role in combating fatigue. A low level of magnesium tends to make a person irritable, nervous, and aggressive, and potassium is required for all muscular activity. Aspartic acid is a "nonessential" amino acid present in asparagus, soybean seeds, young sugar cane, and sugar beet molasses.

My philosophy used to be, "Do something even if it's the wrong thing." I wasted an enormous amount of energy even though I had ample to spare. Now, instead of running ahead, I'm trying to learn to wait on the Lord as suggested in Isaiah 40:31, perhaps the best of all advice:

> Yet those who wait for the Lord
> Will gain new strength;
> They will mount up with wings like eagles;
> They will run and not get tired,
> They will walk and not become weary.

Into a woman's life, particularly, come many opportunities to assist in the care of God's gift of the body. This begins in the mother long before her baby is born. From her children's earliest years, the daily job of physically caring for them is partly her privilege and responsibility. Her attitude toward these precious gifts will likely be that which her children will have toward their own children. As the hub of much home activity, she can help to set a healthy tone for the whole family.

Our physical bodies aren't meant to last forever; like other gifts, they're just "on loan." In spite of all our efforts, accidents occur, eyesights dim, and disease enters in; but sickness or injury can bring unexpected blessings of humbleness, patience, and compassion for others. And most often, we learn how kind and generous other people can be. We are forced to withdraw from activity, and when the pain abates, we marvel at the sheer wasted motion of those around us.

God has a plan in his gift to you of your physical body. It's a sacred gift, this sanctuary where his spirit dwells. Treat it with respect and reverence, and the blessings will flow.

5.

The Gift of Sexuality

Human sexuality is probably one of the most talked about and the least understood of all God's gifts. The more we think we understand it, the more its meaning seems to elude us. The history of male/female relationship is one of abuse, commercialization, exploitation, manipulation, and mass confusion by male and female, among Christians and pagans, with attitudes ranging from hedonism to asceticism.

So many words have been written on the subject of human sexuality that I hesitate to add to their number.* Yet

---

* One of the finest discussions of the general subject of this chapter, as well as Chapter 10, is found in a book by my good friend Jim Reynolds, *Secrets of Eden: God and Human Sexuality* (Austin, TX: Sweet Publishing Co., 1975). The reader is referred to that book, as well as to *All We're Meant to Be* by Letha Scanzoni and Nancy Hardesty (Waco, TX: Word Books, 1974), for a fuller discussion of some of these same ideas.

a study of God's gifts cannot exclude it, for it is close to the heart of our being as humans.

I would prefer looking at broad principles and striking a positive note of celebration for human sexuality to engaging in the controversy that has centered on the degradation of women. Nevertheless, I would like to focus on it long enough to identify some of the problems. Admittedly, both men and women are tragic victims, and both need to be liberated to grow to their full potential. If we're behind in liberating women, we're even further behind in liberating men, because we have hardly begun to look into that subject.

In the beginning

The search for the meaning of human sexuality must begin in the beginning where maleness and femaleness are anchored in God's holy creation. The writer of Genesis stresses that man and woman together are created in the image of God and together receive the vocation to rule over the creation (1:27–31). And God pronounces his creation as being very good. The Genesis writer also stresses the mutual affection and intimacy of these two partners. Woman is created because "it is not good that man should be alone." Her very formation from Adam's rib depicts the affinity between man and woman, and man, recognizing his kinship to her, cries out with rapturous joy, "This at last is bone of my bones and flesh of my flesh" (2:23).

In no way is woman on the same level as the animals; she is not an object of possession and domination for man. She is one flesh with him, a partner suitable for him, a completer; both parts are necessary to make up a whole. Theirs is a sexual union, including both love and reproduction, and an expression involving every fiber of their being. Here we find the ideal of the human couple most clearly stated. When placed in its true context of reverence toward God, this gift of sexuality becomes a celebration in ways that glorify God and bring genuine joy to his sexual creation.

The beginning of the end

How did such mass confusion come out of such a beautiful beginning? What went wrong? And how did it affect our behavior and sexual attitudes in the centuries since that beginning? Let's carefully look again at the Fall.

When Adam and Eve rebelled against God, they sought to become like God, to know good and evil, instead of being subject to God. Their dream gave place to a cruel awareness of their sinful condition. The first sin of Adam and Eve wasn't sexual, but their feelings of shame were somehow bound up with their sexuality and were a token of their lost innocence, of the wound inflicted upon the power of loving. Being no longer truly one with each other or with God, for the first time they knew loneliness.

Here the battle of the sexes began. Like kids caught with their hands in the cookie jar, they blamed everyone but themselves. Adam threw the blame on Eve, and she tried to shift responsibility to the serpent who beguiled her. Their separation from each other and from God was now complete. And ever since, we've been looking in the wrong places to repair the damage.

Though the first sin wasn't sexual in nature, it vitally affected Adam and Eve's male/female relationship. They were no longer completely open to one another in innocence. Because of sin, man was first afflicted with hardship and skimpiness of livelihood. Woman was afflicted with hardship of pregnancy and a profound desire for man. Throughout history, woman has found neither fulfillment nor rest in man but humiliating domination, as God so accurately predicts and describes in Genesis 3:16. Both man and woman have shared the consequence of the first sin. Through disobedience woman became a slave; through disobedience man became a master, ruling over the one whom God gave to him as an equal.

Throughout the Old Testament, the broken sexual relationship is demonstrated in unbridled passions by which man was enslaved. In his effort to satisfy his lust with prostitutes, adulterous love, polygamy, and sexual perversions of all kinds, man allowed human sexuality to become so far removed from its original ideal it's no wonder we fail to recognize it as God intended.

The broken human relationship is inextricably bound up with our relationship with God, and the history of one parallels the history of the other throughout the Old Testament. One notable exception to woman's low position was Deborah. The writer of Judges, in chapters 4 and 5, without elaborate explanation simply tells of her role as wife, prophetess, agitator, ruler, warrior, poetess, and mother. Fifth in line of the leaders (or judges) of Israel whom God himself raised up, she delivered the people from the bondage their idolatry had brought about.

A new beginning

Paradise had virtually disappeared by the time the Old Testament period came to an end. Human relationships had been badly damaged by sin; the result was a world where guilt, shame, and inhuman sexual desires were considered normal behavior. But God in his great love and mercy had been working all along to liberate his creation through the coming of his Son.

By the time Jesus was born into the world, women had suffered hundreds of years of inferiority and humiliation.

The Gift of Sexuality

This was the case even among the Jews, for all of their efforts to be God's people. The morning prayer of the Jewish man, according to Letha Scanzoni and Nancy Hardesty in *All We're Meant to Be*, included thanksgiving that God did not make him a heathen, a slave, or a woman. Bible commentaries, dictionaries, and historians tell us that Jewish custom at this time decreed that no respectable rabbi talked in public with women, and that a Jewish man didn't even speak to his wife, sister, or daughter on the street.

Coming into the world at such a time, Jesus had no regard for such barriers. As pointed out by author Bobbie Lee Holley in an article in *Mission*, "In spite of its long rabbinic tradition, not once did Jesus mention the fall, connect woman with the origin of sin or blame her for all the woman's evils. In fact, the only people he ever railed at for their sinfulness were the hypocritical religious leaders, all of whom were men."[1]

And among the Greeks, woman's only public role was that of the sacred prostitute in pagan temples. Respectable women stayed in their quarters and ate by themselves. They didn't go out alone on the streets or to public assemblies, much less speak in public.

What did Jesus do? While his own disciples marveled, Jesus openly talked with them, healed them, cast out demons, preached to them, forgave them, and wept with them. In short, he treated women as he treated men, as human beings whom he loves even when he seems to be the only one who does.

Ms. Holley points out that we never find Jesus "making jokes about them, lecturing them to stay home where they belong, or even sermonizing about the joys of motherhood." He taught and planted seeds in a generation that wasn't fully aware of their implications. In looking again at all of his relationships with the many women who followed him, I find it amazing to note what he didn't say. My good friend Wes Reagan suggests that the well-known Mary/Martha incident in Luke 10:38–42 was probably more about a woman's place than just a mere kitchen squabble over sharing the chores. And Jesus commended Mary for choosing to sit and learn at his feet rather than fretting about serving dinner.

It is true that, as far as we know, Jesus chose only men as apostles. Whatever his reasons, this seems entirely plausible, for there is a limit to what first-century society would stand for without unnecessarily branding his followers as an immoral group.

As far as I can understand the New Testament, Jesus recognized no double standard of morality, and his ministry, if anything, is a record of liberating men and women from their sins and the sins of inhuman dominion over each other—one race or color over another, male or female, rich or poor, freeman or slave—not because any deserve it, but because of his love. And how we have ever been able to read anything else into the Scriptures seems a mystery.

There is no clearer or more positive statement of liberation for all people of all time than those revolutionary words of the Apostle Paul in Galatians 3:28: "There is neither Jew nor Greek, there is neither slave nor free; there is neither male nor female; for you are all one in Christ Jesus." Spoken to a world steeped in discrimination and prejudice on every one of these levels, these were hard words. And they still give us the same trouble. As Charlotte Bronte wrote in *Jane Eyre*, "Prejudices, it is well known, are most difficult to eradicate from the heart whose soil has never been loosened or fertilized by education; they grow there firm as weeds among stones."

The Gift of Sexuality

The problem of biblical interpretation

How can the Bible seem so revolutionary in one place and so provincial in another? To determine God's eternal principles and his will for us today, we find we must often judge how the words of the New Testament writers were affected by the culture to which they were addressed. Otherwise, the words may seem so contradictory as to lose all meaning and lend themselves to ridicule.

In this context, Paul is a much-talked-about and, I believe, a much-misunderstood man. In a thoroughly male-dominated society, in a world of slaves and social outcasts of all kinds, it is no wonder Paul had difficulty implementing his vision of oneness in Christ. And even Paul himself had trouble understanding what the Spirit inspired him to write. Just as we don't see the Gentiles in the early church for the first ten or twelve years of its life, we don't see women used in certain roles in the church. This isn't even a subject for consideration. To have made it an issue could have been fatally disruptive to the development of the early church. Why else would the same man tell women to keep silent in the churches in 1 Corinthians 14:34, and that women shouldn't teach or exercise authority over a man in 1 Timothy 2:12? Why else would the same Paul who wrote these words of freedom to the Galatians, tell Philemon he's sending back his runaway slave, Onesimus? On and on, the seeming contradictions rage back and forth unless we remember the conditions that existed.

Likewise the Apostle Peter didn't understand the implications of what he was saying through the inspiration of the Spirit. For example, Peter stood up on the day of Pentecost and proclaimed, "For the promise is for you and your children and for all who are far off, as many as the Lord our God shall call to Himself" (Acts 2:39). Yet later, in

Acts 10, the same man didn't seem to know God meant the promise to include the Gentiles, and he had to have that lesson vividly reinforced.

In view of the circumstances, I find it astonishing that in the early life of the church in New Testament times Christian women had been liberated to the point that they were no longer completely isolated from men. Throughout the New Testament we see them functioning as prophetesses, teachers, fellow workers, and servants or deaconesses. The daughters of Philip, the older widows, Phoebe, Priscilla, Lydia, Euodias, Syntyche, and countless others worked and served in areas in a world whose general culture simply didn't allow it, but the church did. Now that is amazing!

We argue back and forth over Scriptures and assume we must reproduce portions of the culture in which the Bible was written, that twentieth-century marital relationships should observe the same hierarchy that existed in the first century. Yet, as Virginia Mollenkott pointed out in her article "The Total Submission Woman," published in *Christian Herald* (Nov. 1975), we don't advocate absolute monarchy or slavery today. Such conditions were present in biblical culture, however, and in some places condoned by Paul as he tried to help the people "adjust to what could not be changed overnight, but eventually would be changed through gospel principles." The same people wouldn't want to go back to monarchy or slavery, but they believe that first-century dominance by men and submission for women should always prevail. Dr. Mollenkott contends they ignore "the fact that both the Old and New Testaments contain visions of radical changes in the sinful social order which would be brought about by obedience to the Good News." They simply can't imagine any other kind of relationship.[2]

It's a real struggle for us to take a fresh look at the

whole tenor of the Bible, to separate what's cultural and what's eternal, instead of going there with our minds already made up. A lot of us do this in considering footwashing, hair lengths, wearing jewelry and veils, the holy kiss, eating meats, observing holidays, circumcision, and so on. Looking at the whole Bible is far more difficult than literalistically citing favorite proof-texts without attention to cultural backgrounds, original languages, and wider scriptural contexts.

It is easy to assume that the injustices of the patriarchal society or of the first century are God's will for all people in all times in all places. When we want easy answers without hard work, let us remember Hosea's cry: "My people are destroyed for lack of knowledge . . ." (Hos. 4:6).

Let's not be afraid really to examine, in context, 1 Corinthians 11, 14; Ephesians 5:22; 1 Timothy 2, 3, 5; Titus 2; and 1 Peter 3:5 and any others that seem to prove dominance and subordination between the sexes. Nor should we neglect the study, again in context, of passages like the following: Hosea 3, 4; Joel 2:28–32; Acts 1:12–14; 2:17–18; 18:26; 21:9; Rom. 16:1–2; 1 Cor. 11:11–12; Gal. 3:28; Eph. 4; 5:21; Phil. 2:3; 4:3; Col. 3; 1 Tim. 3:11; Titus 3; 1 Pet. 2:13; and 1 Pet. 3:7.

Applications and implications

It's obvious how women have suffered, and how women might benefit if we were open enough to face the implications of male/female personhood in God's image, described by Dr. Mollenkott as a relationship of the highest kind between equal but different human beings. How would men benefit? They've been locked into certain roles too. For example, our culture has so overemphasized man's role as breadwinner for the family that he's missed some of the finer points of living. His personal success is often measured by his ability on the job and how much money he makes. The time factor alone hinders him from being the father and husband he may yearn to be. His personal and spiritual growth and his emotional needs are pushed farther back on the shelf.

Some Christian men are aware of the spiritual pitfalls of male supremacy and see the danger that female subservience poses to their own spiritual growth and family happiness. Christian sociologist John Scanzoni believes that power must always be tempered by justice or else it corrupts: "Kings, clergy and presidents with unchecked power become greedy and selfish and exploit others. The same is true of husbands with unchecked power."[3]

I confess I don't know all the ways in which man would benefit personally, but I believe there are many. Freedom tends to scare us. We all want freedom for ourselves, but not for others. Many whites couldn't see how liberating blacks could benefit anyone but the blacks either. Obviously, on the surface, the blacks benefit more, but both eventually will, because it's right. There's a growing recognition that all society suffers when half of it is denied full opportunity for growth, for service, and responsibility.

In an article entitled "Hearken, O Church!" Norman Parks summed it up this way: "Hear, O Church, women are no longer the daughters of Eve, they are the children of God! Men are no longer Baals (Masters), they are husbands (Hosea 2:16). Women are no longer to be subject to the subordination and penalties that followed the Fall, they have been set free! The Serpent is not any longer to bruise their heels, for Christ came to set at liberty them that are bruised. Adam and his peaceable kingdom is the second Eden."[4]

In most male-dominated churches, women are in reality an inferior order of humanity even while lip service is paid to equality. In essence, Dr. Parks says, they are considered

The Gift of Sexuality

to be "equal with men before the throne of grace," but "they are in this life 'subordinate' to men."[5] He suggests that "equal but subordinate" is a contradiction. Subordinate is derived from two Latin words, *sub* (under) and *order* (species), and carries the idea of "inferior" before a "superior." Submission is a good biblical word "which describes the proper relationship of women to men AND men to women." And women to women and men to men! Even then, submission should be freely given and not forced. This is the very core of interpersonal relations within the Christian community; Paul instructs us to submit ourselves "one to another" (Eph. 5:21). People who are equal seek ways to minister to one another. Voluntary submission is not possible until a person is free to make that choice.

As in a democratic society of equals, when for the sake of order, people submit to the ones they elect, no one should regard those who submit as being inferior. The authority is not at all inherent in the one elected but is an authority given for the sake of orderliness. So in the church, the leaders, whether male or female, are by no means of an inherently superior order but hold their positions only to aid orderly spiritual growth and development. Because they lead, they are leaders—not because they have a title.

We've had our view of human sexuality shaped and dominated so long by traditional, historical, and sociological factors that it's about time we put these aside and opened our hearts and hearing anew to what God really has to say on this subject. We like to *talk* about being biblical. It's easier than *being* biblical.

In *Secrets of Eden: God and Human Sexuality,* Jim Reynolds responds seriously to the neglect and abuse of biblical teaching on the subject. He suggests that although most Christians are now aware that man/woman sexual relations are not inherently sinful, several distorted religious views still exist. Speaking to the heart of the matter, he says: "Those who would pray when they need to talk, who would talk of love when they should let love touch, are not godly! . . . Prayer is the atmosphere of sexual intimacy, not a substitute for it."

Another distortion of God's truth is that of identifying lust (evil desire) with God-given sexual desire. Thus, we see married Christians "playing it cool" and obscuring their real interest in sexual relations. The result is a tremendous sexual repression that conflicts with their intended commitment to God.

The healthy (and the biblical) attitude, concludes Dr. Reynolds, begins and ends in a celebration atmosphere: "Disparagement of any part of the body, including the genitals, amounts to attributing evil to the Creator. The circumcised male genital was the sign of God's covenant with Israel, rather than an organ of shame. If anyone desires to attribute evil to any organ of the body, the tongue (James 3), not the genitals, is the most likely candidate."

Despairing strains on the tolerance level

Okay, so I think I've found some answers that seem right for me. What about the strains on my tolerance level? For instance, dirty jokes. American dirty jokes are most often centered on ethnic, racial, or sexual themes. Dr. Joyce Brothers, popular author and psychologist, reported in her syndicated news column that studies have revealed that different nations respond to different types of jokes and people may laugh at the subject about which they have the most anxiety. She pointed out that the French philosopher Henri Bergson believed that in laughter we have always an unavowed intention to humiliate and consequently to correct our neighbor.

Other strains on my tolerance level as a woman are

The Gift of Sexuality

brought about by shallow thinking like that of a preacher who was attempting to prove how "liberation has hurt our women rather than helped them." In an editorial addressed to his Texas Panhandle congregation, "What's Happening to Our Women," he says: "The Biblical admonition is for women to 'dress modestly, with decency and propriety . . . to learn in quietness and full submission.' Paul then adds, 'I do not permit a woman to teach or have authority over a man' (1 Tim. 2:9–12). These principles have been attacked as male chauvinism. Rather, women have been told they are liberated and can do their own thing."

As evidence, he then goes on to quote the "alarming rise" in female crime rates all over the world and comes to this simplistic conclusion: "Women have found that 'Liberation' is not all it's advertised to be." [6]

Statements like these make me want to throw up my hands in despair. I'm reminded of the remark I once heard: "Sometimes we can't tell the truth; it's too confusing." We sure enough can't find the answers if we can't even remember the questions.

Fears and threats

Why is it so hard to conceive of two sexes living together as equals? We surely don't have many models to imitate! Since the Fall, humankind has been hung up on authority and rebellion—in the world, in the nation, in the church, and in the home. For too long we've seen our roles as adult members of society only as imposing some kind of authority or rule on other people, whether as parents, teachers, bosses, or citizens in the community.

Many men feel threatened not only economically but personally by the idea of equality and see it as a move to trespass on their maleness. It's a sad commentary on the human condition that both sexes struggle on the low level of assuming we have to stomp on someone else in order to reach our own highest level of potential. Our self-image is so poor that we think we must climb over the bodies of our own loved ones in order to grow, all the while mouthing the words, "He who would be greatest in the Kingdom of Heaven shall be the servant of all." Lord, but we need your mercy!

And women likewise feel threatened after so many years of hiding in the warm confines of the cozy kitchen or behind the husband's familiar back. The idea of stepping out into the blinding light of freedom and taking on the responsibility of a whole person, while exhilarating to some, is horrifying to others. Trying to follow the traditional role has not made me whole. It only gave me delusions of security, but like the ostrich with his head stuck in the sand, the rest of me remained pitifully exposed to the elements.

If I fear anything, it is not that we'll become whole people. Rather, women may prostitute themselves to get into positions of power to right the wrongs and forget what they set out to do—to make right relationships between men and women. Philosopher George Santayana once defined fanaticism as "redoubling your efforts when you have forgotten your aim."[7] Lord, help us from becoming fanatics in that sense. It is my prayer that our aim may not be forgotten and that it won't become irrelevant. If our ministry is not one of making *all* people whole, I question both its validity and its success, and I want no part in it.

To become whole again we don't need weaker sexual desires or better marriage laws. What both men and women need is first to repair the broken relationship with their Creator; then they can turn to the task of repairing the broken relationship between his creatures.

It's time to call off the war. We need each other. And baby, we've come a long way since the Fall, but we've got a long way to go. In our instantism culture, it's hard to muster patience as we all learn to accept our true selves and each other as created equals that God made in the beginning.

Fear of change

We can't change things by just rearranging the furniture. Change does not necessarily produce growth, though growth produces change. It has to come from within; it can't be legislated. The head doesn't hear anything until the heart has listened.

What are we afraid of? "Fear of change is a threat, for if we open ourselves to new experience and thus allow for change to occur, we must in that opening give up control. That is precisely what we have steeled ourselves against for many years," says George Isaac Brown in his book *Human Teaching for Human Learning.* He goes on to suggest that one way we avoid change is by creating with our minds imaginary catastrophes that might happen if we were to move into the unknown realm of new experience. When this happens we are out of touch with our own strength and resources. We need each other, but it's absurd and wasteful to believe that we need others to do things we are perfectly capable of doing ourselves—to refuse to take responsibility for ourselves and for what we do or could do.[8]

Jess Lair, in my opinion one of the courageous thinkers of our time, speaks to the subject of change in his first book. *I Ain't Much, Baby—But I'm All I've Got.* He compares change to the way a snake sheds his skin. "The snake doesn't shed his skin until he's got a full new one grown underneath. And when he's got a full new one underneath, the old one just falls away." You can't force change, Dr. Lair believes, and our lives aren't going to change just because we see some things wrong with them. But it happens gradually and steadily, so much so it looks as if change sneaks up on us. Then one day we recognize, "Hey, I lost my old skin." He concludes: "It just fell away because I didn't need it anymore." I think that's a beautiful process, and it happens when and only when we don't need that old skin anymore.[9]

What we need

A more open atmosphere is what I need in my identity search. Inward freedom is too powerful to remain hidden for long, and change will ultimately be outward as well as inward. Who am I, and who are you? And what is our role before God? Just as tight shoes will stunt the growth of a child's feet, so can a tight arena stunt the growth of people. Both sexes need more room to wiggle their toes!

Going against one's background and even the mainstream of religious thought can be very painful. But as the French novelist and essayist André Gide once said: "Man cannot discover new oceans unless he has the courage to lose sight of the shore."

The road back

How do we get from where we are to where we need to be? I don't know what the future holds for male/female relationships, nor how many steps forward we can take without having to take a step backwards, but I'm excited. I see signs of progress. George Santayana advised, "We must welcome the future, remembering that soon it will be the past; and we must respect the past, knowing that once it was all that was humanly possible." Even so, for some of us the future's going to arrive before we're ready to give up the present.

The Gift of Sexuality

Since the male/female relationship was broken and marred when Adam and Eve first sinned, it would appear that though conditions may worsen or improve from time to time, the bridge cannot be perfectly repaired until eternity. But just as we strive for sinless perfection even while knowing we sin, we must also strive for wholeness in other ways. Our human sexuality is God's gift. Our frustration is not having anyone to blame but ourselves.

In the words of poet T. S. Eliot,

> We shall not cease from exploration
> And the end of all our exploring
> Will be to arrive where we started
> And know the place for the first time.[10]

6.

The Gift of Money and Possessions

Preachers have probably preached on the subject of money and possessions more than on all God's other gifts, and perhaps rightly so, for it pinpoints one of our biggest hang-ups. The Bible is a book on giving, much of it concerning our miserly attitudes toward our money and possessions. I confess that my wealth is the most difficult gift God has given me. At best I only manage to feel I'm not falling behind.

Wealth is a relative term

Money is simply a medium of exchange that represents our time and abilities in a negotiable form, yet economics, world banking, and high finance are so complicated that the average person can hardly understand them without special training.

The Gift of Money and Possessions

One day our older son, Kyle, who was ten years old at the time, after hearing his father make such a statement in a sermon, asked me, "Mom, are we really rich?" We looked it up in the dictionary and found that rich means abundant and valuable possessions. "And how much money do we have?" he asked. We checked the contents of my billfold ($1.35) and our latest bank statement ($155.19). "That's all we have, and we're rich?"

I tried to explain in terms he could understand that while we had little money, we were rich because we had great possessions. We owned a car, some furniture and appliances, and many books. Seeing that this didn't impress him, I told him about income potential. We had good health, strong bodies, and an education that would permit us to do many things to earn money. It still didn't sound like much to him, however, because he knew someone much richer. Somehow we always manage to weasel out of feeling we're rich because we always know someone who has more.

My father died when I was seven years old, leaving a widow and four girls. We often had struggles just to eat, but I didn't feel poor because I didn't know anyone with much more. Twelve years later I worked as a secretary in an organization supported by a man who was declared to be the richest man in the world. I earned more money than I've ever earned in proportion to my expenses, and yet I felt very poor.

But when I lived in Brazil, I knew what it was to be rich. Our neighborhood was middle-class, but in terms of possessions and education, we were the wealthiest family on the block. It was hard to know how to respond to friends in the States who lovingly sent us "some essentials." By American standards we were sacrificing a great deal because we couldn't buy most canned goods, plastic bags, and aged beef; had to drink filtered or bottled water; and rinsed our fresh vegetables in a weak bleach solution to kill the parasites.

Since our return, I've become used to affluence again, but my conscience nips at me when I throw out some molded bread or leftover leftovers. I can't forget the beggars who daily made the rounds of my garbage can in Brazil, and who eagerly fed on such scraps as orange peelings and rotten bananas or some old soup bones. And I don't want to forget.

Somewhat like the Apostle Paul, I've known a little bit of what it's like to be rich and to be poor, and I think it's a whole lot more comfortable in spirit to be poor. It's a severe test for me to live for God in the midst of such abundance. As Kirk, our younger son, once said when I was reminding him to spend his money wisely, "Aw, Mom, it was easy for you to learn the value of a dollar when you were a kid. You didn't have one."

Affluence is a new thing

John Kenneth Galbraith tells us that, from the earliest of times down to the beginning of the eighteenth century, people of the world saw no great change in their standard of living; only in the last few generations, in a small corner of the world, have we experienced affluence in wealth. But such great and unprecedented affluence has not made us more content. No one quite knows what to do with his or her wealth. "The poor man," Galbraith said, "has always a precise view of his problem and its remedy: He hasn't enough and he needs more. The rich man can imagine a much greater variety of ills and he will be correspondingly less certain of their remedy." [1]

Yet in the midst of such affluence, most of us unbelievably feel the pressure of never having quite enough money. Our song is, "My name's Jimmy. I'll take all you'll gimme."

The Gift of Money and Possessions

When my husband I were both struggling through our first college years, one of our good friends used to say that if he ever had a lot of money, he'd never be selfish with it. Then his father died and left him a very small inheritance. He said he began to be greedy and wanted even more. It scared him so much that he put it in a special account to give away, and for several years we received a monthly check from him to use in our work in Brazil.

I used to think that most of the people we knew had very little money until we raised funds for our work in Brazil. As the money poured in, I couldn't believe the wealth and abundance of our friends. The money is there when we decide what we want to do with it.

The words of Moses haunt me. He warned the children of Israel when they came to the promised land: "[Take heed] lest when you have eaten and are satisfied, and have built good houses and lived in them, and when your herds and your flocks multiply, and your silver and gold multiply, and all that you have multiplies, then your heart becomes proud, and you forget the Lord your God who brought you out from the land of Egypt, out of the house of slavery" (Deut. 8:12–14). It's so easy for us to say, as God said we might, "My power and the strength of my hand made me this wealth" (v. 17).

The use of riches

Many people have told me, "Ah, but it's easier for you, being a minister's wife. You can understand the idea of being a steward of your money because your income is from money people gave to the Lord." But it's not a bit easier when my husband is paid as a minister or as a history or psychology professor!

A necessity is an urgent need, something indispensable to life. Everyone agrees a person needs to buy the necessities of life, but the Madison Avenue merchandisers have done such a good job of creating appetites that we seem to need everything. It's hard to remember that our forefathers did without sugar until the thirteenth century; without coal fires until the fourteenth; without buttered bread until the sixteenth; tea or soap until the seventeenth; without gas, matches or electricity until the nineteenth; without cars, canned or frozen foods until the twentieth.

My husband has notes in his files telling of a survey that was made in 1868, in which it was found that the American people had 19 necessities and 56 wants. But 100 years later, in 1968, the list had grown to 94 necessities and 390 wants! We Americans are not lukewarm wanters. Whether these figures are exact or not, I know my own needs have grown considerably since the years when I had only one pair of shoes because I had only one pair of feet—and went barefoot in the summer to save them for school.

In another survey, in 1975, the Institute of Life Insurance asked people between the ages of fourteen and twenty-five to rank items according to their essential needs of the future. In order of preference, they listed home ownership, a pension plan, a savings account of at least $5,000, life insurance totaling at least $50,000, a college education, a new car, an air-conditioned home, opportunities for travel abroad, a stereo system, a master's degree, a color TV set, and a dishwasher.[2] Wow! Now that's some list of essentials.

So what's a luxury? By definition, it's free indulgence; anything that gratifies the appetite; a mode of life characterized by material abundance. By practice we all know it's something we want so badly that it soon becomes a necessity. What was impossible yesterday becomes a luxury today and a necessity tomorrow.

The Gift of Money and Possessions

Am I more Christlike if I have a smaller amount of money and possessions? Or less, if I have great wealth? I wish it were that simple, but there's no special virtue in wearing a hair shirt and eating wild locusts and honey. My problem lies not with the thousands I don't have, but in my stinginess with the dollar I do.

But isn't there a limit to the number of luxuries that I can conscientiously possess? Definitely. I know where my limit is, I think, but only you can determine yours. My luxury might be your necessity, and vice versa. For example, labor-saving devices have always been high on my list of necessities because they free me to do other work a machine can't do. A friend of mine says he knows from experience how much happier and productive he is when he's in comfortable and pleasant surroundings; he'll sacrifice something else in order to afford a nice home, so he contentedly drives a car held together with chewing gum and baling wire.

My husband and I have always had money for college tuition and a good typewriter when we didn't have wall-to-wall floors and the sun woke us up coming through the nail holes in our thin plywood walls. But we could always buy books. Besides being necessary tools to help me grow, my books speak to me. And though I live in a small house, books provide a kind of window on the world.

I recently mentioned a certain book I was reading as I sat down to a gourmet meal in a beautiful home and heard the hostess wistfully say, "I just can't afford to buy books. They're so expensive these days." What she meant was, "I don't choose to spend my money that way." And that's legitimate.

Although I understand men traditionally buy most of the cars, boats, tools, and sports equipment, ad men judge that women do 85 to 90 percent of the buying for the family, and they plan their ads to catch the female eye. We buy for ourselves, our children, our husbands, our homes, and everything in them. And then we have to buy all that equipment and supplies necessary to care for the possessions we've just bought. A friend of mine once said that every time she was tempted to buy a new piece of furniture, all she had to do was visualize the hours required to keep it dusted and cleaned. The mental picture of having to pack and unpack something every time I move has often kept my money in my pocket.

Money nerves

Some of us would be willing to live like poor men if we just had the security of knowing we had a great deal of money. We're a lot like Joe Louis, who once said, "It isn't that I like money so much, but it sure calms my nerves." Yet people I've seen who have a lot of money aren't free people; they still have money nerves. Money does little to calm us down, and yet we continue to fall into the trap of thinking we need money for security.

I think it gets harder for me to be generous as I grow older. After I hit forty years of age, I found, for the first time, periods during which my physical energy was diminishing. It's a humbling experience to a brash, energetic person like me. And though my energy to make money may decrease, in my more thoughtful moments I know I'm still too rich for my own good.

I don't know why I am so selfish when I know I can't possibly outgive God. My older son, Kyle, who's always seeking ways to multiply his income, asked me one day, "Does the Lord really promise you'll receive more if you give more?" We opened the Bible and read Ecclesiastes 11:1: "Cast your bread on the surface of the waters, for

The Gift of Money and Possessions

you will find it after many days." We talked about the law of return, and that when you give something to the Lord, it'll come back to you. If you want to keep it, you give it away. It was interesting to see my son, who was enjoying calculus and trigonometry that year, as he wrestled with this concept.

And then we opened to Malachi 3:10, and I think it's significant that the last book of the Old Testament speaks these words: "Bring the whole tithe into the storehouse, so that there may be food in My house and test Me now in this," says the Lord of hosts, "if I will not open for you the windows of heaven, and pour out for you a blessing until there is no more need." He really dares us, doesn't he?

Enjoy your money

One of my favorite American authors is Willa Cather. In her short story "Neighbour Rosicky," she tells how everyone's corn crop was burned up by the hot wind one year in Nebraska. All of the neighbors were so discouraged they couldn't look anyone in the face—except for Rosicky and his family. His wife's comment was, "An' we enjoyed ourselves that year, poor as we was, an' our neighbours wasn't a bit better off for bein' miserable. Some of 'em grieved till they got poor digestions and couldn't relish what they did have." If I could have grown up in Neighbour Rosicky's family, maybe I could stop wishing for things long enough to enjoy what I do have.

I like what Charlie Shedd said in *You Can Be a Great Parent* about teaching his children to give a tenth, save a tenth, and enjoy the rest. I know that God gave us these gifts, just as he has with all our other gifts, not to guard and save, but to use joyfully—whether we call our bank to get our balance or just shake ours.

And enjoy giving it away

Dr. Karl Menninger of the Menninger Clinic in Topeka once said, "Money-giving is a good criterion of a person's mental health. Generous people are rarely mentally ill people." Why? Because of what it does for the giver. Maybe that's what Jesus was trying to say to the rich, young ruler in Matthew 19 when he told him to sell all he had and give it to the poor. He wasn't concerned with the money, but with the young man.

The first time I ever felt just a little bit of the truth in the words "it's more blessed to give than receive" was in reverse order. A widow once gave us $250 to "spend on ourselves," and knowing some of her hardships through the years, we had a hard time enjoying it. We'd visited in her little home several times; it was bare of so many items I considered necessities. We tried to accept her gift of love graciously. You know, I can't remember what we spent the money for, but I can plainly see the radiance in her tiny, wrinkled face.

Paul tells us in 2 Corinthians 8 about the strange churches in Macedonia who begged to help participate in his work. I don't know if I've ever seen anyone beg to be able to give, and Paul seems to think it was rather unexpected too. But he drops this key phrase: ". . . but they first gave themselves to the Lord . . ." (v. 5).

It's not the amount that counts

In his autobiography, *Up from Slavery,* Booker T. Washington tells of the many people who gave to help the cause of education. One was an old, crippled black woman, clad in rags, who hobbled into the room one day and said: "Mr. Washington, God knows I spent de bes' days of my life in slavery. God knows I's ignorant an' poor; but I knows

The Gift of Money and Possessions

what you an' Miss Davidson is trying to do. I knows you is tryin' to make better men and better women for de coloured race. I ain't got no money but I wants you to take dese six eggs, what I's been savin' up, an' I wants you to put dese six eggs into the eddication of dese boys an' gals." [3] The dialect may be quaint today, but the feeling is there. Six eggs don't sound like much, but Washington said that of all the many gifts he received, none touched him so deeply as this.

It's not how much I give, but how much I give of what I've got. Our finest example is the poor widow that Jesus praised who put in two mites. She gave the smallest legal amount she could give as a Jew. Her gift represented almost nothing. But it was all she had, all of her living. I've never come close to that kind of giving, and I've never known anyone who has.

And to top it off, we are warned in 1 Corinthians 13 that if we give away all we have and even deliver our body to be burned, and have not love, we are nothing. That's the *pièce de résistance*. Giving must be done in love or it doesn't count.

I think sometimes we have so sterilized our giving that we miss a lot of the joy. We tend to think giving to the Lord means dropping a little money in the collection plate on Sunday morning. But giving is much, much broader than that.

Jess Lair understands real giving more than any man I've ever known. In his third book, *I Ain't Well—But I Sure Am Better*, he tells us the things that mean so much to him are the ones that have been given to him. "Those things I gave away were very sweet because they meant much more to me than the three or four things I kept for myself." [4] Jess knows the giver is the one who benefits the most, and everything we have is given to us, so the faster we can give it all away the better.

I don't know why the Lord has given me so much, but I want to know the joy of contentment in poverty or riches. I want honestly to confront Jesus' words: "For where your treasure is, there will your heart be also." I don't want to forget the lesson of the parable of the talents—that if I don't use the blessing of my wealth it's likely to be taken away. But that's such a negative approach. I'd prefer to have higher aims.

My goal is to be like King David, who refused to offer burnt offerings to the Lord which cost him nothing (2 Sam. 24:24). But the Lord knows I am such a sinner, for I know I have great possessions.

As Jess Lair said, "The only way to teach generosity is by being generous. If I'm generous, I don't need to talk about it. If I'm not generous, look how awful it is to preach to my kids about how they should be generous." [5]

7.

The Gift of Happiness

Happiness is an emotion we don't seem to recognize while we're happy but can remember all too clearly when we're not. Some of us begin each day with a frantic search for happiness as if we were responding to the well-known TV commercial that proposed we only go around once in life so we should give it all the gusto we've got. Others take a more passive approach; like Charlie Brown, they sit under a tree and wonder if happiness will come their way today. One man I know successfully uses a kind of backhand method. He says he believes you shouldn't expect happiness; that if you would only recognize life is hard, things would be so much easier for you.

Joseph Addison believed that the grand essentials to happiness were something to do, something to love, and something to hope for. English novelist Norman Douglas declared the secret of happiness was curiosity, and Scottish playwright James Barrie said, "The secret of happiness is not in doing what one likes but in liking what one has to do."

Happiness sounds simple enough. So what's the problem? Never have so many citizens of any society achieved such dreams as Americans enjoy. And never have so many spent so much money on recreation and leisure and escapism in search of happiness. Yet the best of times seems the worst of times, for the American Medical Association says there are some ten million Americans needing treatment for depression, and psychiatric treatment for children is rising at an alarming rate.

Work used to be a divine privilege and the source of much happiness, but the American Management Association reports absenteeism and career dissatisfaction are at an alarming high point. Could the seventeenth-century writer La Rouchefoucauld have known about us when he said this: "Few things are needed to make the wise man happy, but nothing satisfies the fool—and this is the reason why so many of mankind are miserable." [1]

American women are the envy of women throughout the world for the comparative freedom and opportunity we have to do what we want. We strive for success in marriage, motherhood, homemaking; and, more and more, we try to combine these with an outside job. Some of us think we want a vine-covered cottage and kids, only to discover that when we're doing the housewife bit, we can't wait to step back into the bustling world again. I believe our unhappiness results from our unrealistic standards, for our model is a myth. We tend to measure our success and happiness by comparing ourselves, not to real people like family, neighbors, and friends, but to women on television who are always beautifully groomed, who have spotless kitchens and well-behaved children. We think we should be much more than we are and have much more than we have. (We fail to realize, however, that no one can be a complete success or be completely happy in so many demanding areas of life.)

If we observe very many of those around us, it is hard to deny that we're a bunch of unhappy people, usually looking for happiness in all the wrong places. Not everyone needs Linus's security blanket for happiness, but most of us obviously think we need something other than what we've got to make us happy. We are like the people being addressed in Haggai 1:6: "You have sown much, but harvest little; you eat, but there is not enough to be satisfied; you drink, but there is not enough to become drunk; you put on clothing, but no one is warm enough; and he who earns, earns wages to put into a purse with holes."

Novelist Flannery O'Connor, in *Mystery and Manners*, describes modern man or woman as one who "wanders about, caught in a maze of guilt he can't identify, trying to reach a God he can't approach, a God powerless to approach him. And there is another type of modern man who can neither believe nor contain himself in unbelief and who searches desperately, feeling about in all experience for the lost God." Her conclusion says it all: "At its best our age is an age of searchers and discoverers, and at its worst, an age that has domesticated despair and learned to live with it happily." [2]

Looking inward, I think I identify most with Charlie Brown, as do so many others who've made him famous. His creator, Charles Schulz, explains him as "everybody who ever ran the wrong way on a football field, missed home plate on the winning run, or ran out of gas in the home stretch." He says Charlie is basically an optimist, but he prefers to call him an "optimistic failure." [3]

Still, although I can read about all of the things that happiness is or is not for others, until I know my own happiness, these are just words. And the words of others don't always help much. For instance, I wrote some of this chapter a few days ago when I was feeling extremely elated. But as I revise it now—several days later on a rather everydayish day—it sounds rather glib and unreal to me, and I wonder how much its helpfulness will depend on your mood when you read it.

So I can only tell you how it is with me; your own happiness is up to you. I do believe that God has given you and me all of the tools we need for happiness, that our happiness is directly linked to knowing who you and I are as children of God, where we're going, and what it's all about. I have come to know personally that, as Corrie ten Boom said in *The Hiding Place*, "Happiness isn't something that depends on our surroundings. It's something we make inside ourselves." I've begun to realize that happiness, like love, is sometimes an emotion, but basically it's a decision. I decide to be happy and even when I don't have that feeling very strongly today, it's still there deep inside, and I know I'll experience it again tomorrow or the day after.

I believe David must have tasted depression as much as anyone because he talked about happiness so much. The Book of Psalms opens with these words: "Happy are those who reject the advice of evil men, who do not follow the example of sinners or join those who have no use for God" (Ps. 1:1, TEV). He goes on to describe the happy person as like "the trees that grow beside a stream, that bear fruit at the right time, and whose leaves do not dry up" (Ps. 1:3, TEV). As I look out my window and see nothing but gray rain, I wonder if maybe Psalm 118:24 was written on just such a gloomy day as this: "This is the day which the Lord has made; let us rejoice and be glad in it" (RSV).

I know that my happiness can't depend on how great I am as a wife, a teacher, or a writer, as a mother or a mender of torn blue jeans. I'm never going to be that great at anything I do. Happiness is something much broader than that. I believe Jess Lair spoke truly in *"I Ain't Much, Baby—But I'm All I've Got,"* when he said, "Happiness has got nothing to do with the so-called status or size of the profession. It's got something to do with size of the person who's in the profession and the heart of the person who's in that profession." [4]

Peace and contentment don't come when I've cleared up all of the conflicts in my life, but when I've learned to cope with them. Jess Lair says that "the secret is to change everything in my life that I can't accept and then accept everything I can't change." So the quest continues throughout life: What can't I accept? How can I change it? Then, how do I go about accepting the residue?

The good life exists for me when I stop wanting a better one because the itch for things drains my soul of contentment. I know I'll never earn enough, and the house will never be furnished just right. I'll never love enough or know enough. But there comes a time when I have to step off this merry-go-round of discontentment and say: "That's it! What I have will do."

Being content is like forever living on a mountain. I've always loved the mountains, and some of my calmest moments of ecstasy have been at ten thousand feet. At that height, I gain a perspective I lack on the low plains, and little things don't seem so big up there, surrounded by such grandeur. Even other mountains around me don't seem so formidable, and the valleys below are mere shadows in the distance. Up there I feel only the brilliance of the sun on my face, and there's absolute stillness and peace. And it is enough.

As I grow older, I believe more and more that life is simply too short to spend in pursuit of the wrong things. I echo Solzhenitsyn's question in *The Gulag Archipelago*, "If in order to live, it is necessary not to live, then what's it all for?"[5]

God offers us power for abundant living. I believe that's a close kin to happiness. "[He] is able to do exceeding abundantly beyond all that we ask or think, according to the power that works within us" (Eph. 3:20). Someone once suggested, "Let the redeemed show they've been redeemed and more will be willing to listen to our Redeemer." If we could do that, people would be tapping us on the shoulder and saying, "Hey there, I could use a little of that in my life. How do I get it?"

Happiness may have little to do with my salvation, but it helps me enjoy it more. It's like having my cake and eating it too. It isn't found in possessions, success, or good or bad health, but in the union of myself with God. It's only found when I'm in step with God, when my spirit is attune with his spirit. Whatever my burden, if I can look toward the light, the shadow of it falls behind me.

I find that I'm happy to a great extent because I expect to be, and that provides a kind of insulation. William James advised, "Be not afraid of life. Believe that life is worth living and your belief will help create the fact."[6] And in a *Parade* magazine interview actress Doris Day said she determined after her husband died that she was going to be like those little clown dolls that are round on the bottom, because with a round bottom you can't get knocked down. She declared that, "Today I've got a round, round bottom. I just know that whatever is happening is going to be good."

Believing that something good is going to happen to me may sometimes be little more than whistling in the dark, but it helps sustain me. People have asked me, "How can you write about such pleasant things when there's so much trouble in the world?" Maybe it's because of a quote

The Gift of Happiness

I came across a long time ago that has become my touchstone. Translated, the words written in 1513 by Fra Giovanni tell us: "The gloom of the world is but a shadow. Behind it, yet within reach, is joy. There is a radiance and glory in the darkness could we but see, and to see we have only to look. I beseech you to look!" [7]

Gary Player used to tell people what he thought of their golf courses when he was on tour. But it got everyone so upset that he began to say they've all got the greatest courses in the world. The surprising thing was that it helped him. He said, "If I think the course is lousy, I play lousy golf. But if I convince myself it's great, I don't spend my time out there thinking how bad it is." [8]

The world certainly has enough people who tell it like it is; we could use a few more who can tell it like it can be. One of my prized possessions is a framed quotation from the musical *Man of La Mancha:* "Too much sanity may be madness. And the maddest of all, to see life as it is and not as it should be." [9]

While I'm basically a happy person, I have an occasional period when I'm not, and that hurts me because I feel it's such a waste! It's something I'm trying to change in my life and trying to accept when I can't change it.

It was a long time before I admitted I had to expect periods of unhappiness in my life. Maybe it's for the reason that Kahlil Gibran suggested in *The Prophet,* that joy and sorrow are inseparable. "Your joy is your sorrow unmasked. And the selfsame well from which your laughter rises was oftentimes filled with your tears." [10]

Over the years, I've collected so many bits and pieces of advice on overcoming depression that the manila folders into which I've thrown them now occupy almost a foot of filing space. I wish I knew of a crash course in serenity I could recommend, but the best I can come up with is a series of steps that I go through, operating on the principle that "doing beats stewing." I find they sometimes get my adrenalin flowing again.

1. I look at the things that have often given me joy in the past. This only works if I'm feeling just a little low. But it's worth a try. At least it acts as a barometer of the level of my unhappiness.

There are many good things that have come my way, and looking at these help me savor what is, rather than longing for what might be. I have a special section in my happiness file with mementos and notes that I've jotted down. These may be letters from readers, honors I've received, pictures of our family on an outing in the country, or quotations or articles I like. There's a note with these words: "Mom, you're the bestest cook in the world!" That was said by our younger son, Kirk, at age four. When my husband, Robert, said, "The only real intelligent decision I ever made was to marry you," it went in the folder too. I call it my "What-you-have-is-what-it-takes-file."

If this doesn't boost my self-image and lift my depression, I quickly move on to something else. Dwelling on this only makes me feel worse because I know I'm not appreciating my blessings.

2. I look for something to do that's physically tiring. I once saw a poster with these words by L. Richard Lessor: "Happiness is like a butterfly. The more you chase it, the more it will elude you. But if you turn your attention to other things, it comes and softly sits on your shoulder." Anyhow, digging in the garden or scrubbing the woodwork gives me a certain puritanical feeling. And even if I don't enjoy it, if it's something I've wanted to get done for a long while, that's a plus. Jogging or tennis can also tire my bones so that I have a reason to feel tired and can fall right to sleep that night.

3. I remind myself that I just have to get through today,

that I'll feel better tomorrow—because I always have. Sure, I don't remember what it's like to be happy right now, but I know I have been because I've actually written down the dates in my journal. It takes an awful lot of courage just to hold onto that sometimes, but facing the next five minutes is the worst.

Sometimes it seems impossible to think in these terms. I remember what Lewis Carroll's character, the Queen of Hearts, said in *Alice in Wonderland:* "I dare say you haven't had much practice. When I was your age I always did it for an half-an-hour-a-day. Why, sometimes I've believed as many as six impossible things before breakfast."

So when I think of all the sentence fragments and fused sentences I'll have to correct on essays of college freshmen, the number of peanut butter and jelly sandwiches I'll make, or all the dirty socks I'll wash and put away, I can't face them. But by looking at them one day at a time, the job is bearable.

4. I even keep some jokes or humorous material around to read on bleary days. Laughter, like tears, serves as a catharsis. Maybe that's what one of Jess Lair's students meant when he wrote: "He who laughs, lasts." [11] And some people say reading a sad book or seeing a sad movie will allow them a good cry, and that gets them going again.

5. Sometimes, I'm just plain weary, so I go to bed.

6. I do something unexpected and outrageous. The more so the better. It helps me get my mind off myself. Some people feel the surest way to puncture a pleasure is to overanticipate it, and that the best things in life are not free but unexpected. I may read a novel just for fun at ten o'clock in the morning. Or go out on the town in the middle of the week. That might not sound like much to you, but to a country girl who was taught to work while the sun is still high and go to town on Saturday night, it's outrageous.

Eda LeShan, an exceptional writer and family-life specialist, said in a *Woman's Day* article that her life was never the same after she had hamburgers for breakfast for the first time. Why not? It's as good protein-wise as bacon and eggs. Or when it's hot and you're looking for a breakfast of fruit, milk, and cereal, you can find the same ingredients in a strawberry ice cream cone. Ms. LeShan says whenever she finds herself "behaving in rigid ways, becoming inflexible and unquestioning about rules and regulations," she whispers to herself, "Hamburgers for breakfast." [12]

I too need to get rid of the "shoulds" and "oughts" in my life once in awhile: I need to stay up for the late, late show, stuff myself with junk at the beach, or slip off with just my husband for a long weekend. Ms. LeShan's antidote for those hysterical moments in life include a run in the warm summer rain with your clothes on, ending up with "a dance across the yard." One of the reasons she became a writer was, she says, "because once, when I was driving home with my parents, they let me keep a date with a rainbow. There had been a heavy summer storm, when suddenly I screamed, 'Stop the car. I must write a poem about that beautiful rainbow!' " Such special moments are what spontaneity and joy are all about.

Some of my happiest moments have had something to do with the unexpected. I remember an outing in the park along Red River in Fargo, North Dakota, when we roasted wieners and marshmallows and piled up autumn leaves and took turns jumping into the heap, yelling, "Geronimo!" I can still taste the loaf of homemade bread I once took out of the oven in our Oregon home, past bedtime. We put another log of applewood on the fire and ate hot slices of whole-wheat bread while the butter dripped all over our clean pajamas.

7. But sometimes none of these ideas work, so I chuck everything and just give in to my depression. I take the

day off and do nothing but putter around. I follow my nose, much like the kids who wander around in the middle of summer when they're burned out on swimming, baseball, and television, and wail, "There's absolutely nothing to do." Going out into God's world often rekindles my fire, so I deliberately look for something in nature. I may water the garden, check the cedars for bagworms, or watch the red maple leaves dance in the wind. Once while looking for ripe tomatoes, the very smell of the vines was so heavenly that I spent the rest of the day lying in a recliner on the patio, digging into those memories of the farm when I walked barefooted in the evening with my father down by the creek to our tomato patch. I can still smell it. It was a memory I thought was lost, but it surfaced and was important to me somehow.

In fact, this idea of a nature walk came to me by accident on just such an occasion when I was grumbling around one day and saw some butterflies rising up together from a lilac bush. I recalled how, when I was in Vernon High School, I used to have a long walk back and forth to school. I'd see something beautiful, and the feeling of it would last me throughout any trying moments during the day. Even when I saw my best friend trying to steal my boyfriend, it helped my spirits to recall the birds who had bathed in a rain puddle that morning, or the sun shining through the cottonwood trees making the leaves dance a jig. I've continued to experience similar brief periods of great joy since those high school days, but I'd never realized where they came from until twenty years later in my backyard in Manhattan, Kansas.

If I've gone through my whole list and nothing has seemed to work, enough time has usually passed that I've managed to live through my depression. Indeed, time is often just what I need.

Happiness is a very personal, private thing. We are constantly called upon to create our own happiness. Our happiness shows our uniqueness as much as anything else. Many disagree on what brings happiness, but almost all of us have experienced the miracle of finding ourselves suddenly happy. Nothing has changed. Nothing is different, but everything seems so. There's a soundless click, and for one brief shining moment, we are in Camelot. And we know it's a gift from God.

8.

The Gift of Time

Unlike what he has done with many of our other gifts, the Lord gives us all the same gift of time. Everyone has days with twenty-four hours, the only difference being the number of days he's given us. Ralph Waldo Emerson observed: "God had infinite time to give us; but how did He give it? In one immense tract of lazy millenniums? No, He cut it up into a neat succession of new mornings."

In a Houston newspaper interview, Dr. John McGovern, a well-known medical doctor, teacher, researcher, and author, said of his busy life: "My philosophy is that the best chance of a good tomorrow is a day well-lived. But it's hard to do—to put a curtain on yesterday and all its failures and bring all efforts to bear on today, whether it's work or play. Most people worry about the failures of yesterday and what's coming up tomorrow and never live today." [1]

The average person thinks it's a good idea but tends to drift through life. One day spills over into the next until another week, another month, and then another year has gone by. Sure, we may work at a job from 8 to 5, but life seems to be slipping by, and we don't seem to get anything of importance done. We tend to live our lives about the way we watch TV: the program's not very good, but we're too lazy to get up and change it.

A bad odor often surrounds those who do. *Time nuts,* we call them. They become so overwhelmingly occupied with time and work, they're a study in tragicomedy—always making, updating, losing, and remaking their lists. Lacking spontaneity and flexibility, they never relax and are always nervously fretting and fuming. Who wants to be around people like that, much less be like that? And heaven help the poor soul who's married to a time nut.

What I strive for is neither extreme. Making the most of our gift of time is a matter of balance. All of us require different degrees of structure and spontaneity in our lives, and we have different needs at different ages and at different times of the year. At some periods in my life I've had to throw out all my plans and hang loose while I found myself again. But the more control I achieve over my days, the greater freedom and the more serenity I experience, and that's something to work for.

My problems in achieving this balance are many:

The days are frittered away by detail. I feel picked on by everyone because everyone seems to want some of my time. A babel of voices surrounds me.

Anne Morrow Lindbergh, in *Gift from the Sea,* describes the life of the American housewife as "a whole caravan of complications." She likens her to the circus trapeze artists who "run a tight rope daily, balancing a pile of books on the head" while engaging in a never-ending stream of activities. Hers is "not the life of simplicity but the life of multiplicity that wise men warn us of." [2]

The Gift of Time

Someone once said that keeping house is like stringing beads, but with no knot in the end of the string. No wonder we feel that the day is done before we are. As Seneca said a long time ago, "Part of our time is snatched away from us, part is gently subtracted, and part slides insensibly away."

Snoopy said he once felt like running away when he was at the Daisy Hill Puppy Farm. "I climbed over the fence," he said, "but I was still in the world." Well, sometimes I'd like to pull my blouse up over my head and hide out in a cave somewhere. But if I can't run away, or stick my head in the sand, then I must simplify my life.

Thoreau's solution was to spend some two years in a hut he built for $28.125. I've never been able to achieve that Walden Pond level of austerity, but reading about it calms me down some and helps to simplify my own life in suburbia.

Others spend my time for me. I have to learn to say no quickly and firmly but calmly and not feel guilty or obliged to justify my refusal. I believe everyone has the same right to refuse that the other person has to ask, if not more. But I must be willing to take the consequences of that action.

The world abounds with good causes, and I think Christians have often been caught in the trap of helping every good cause that knocks on the door. But I can't do what *I* feel is important if I let myself be talked into doing other things. If I refuse without impatience or anger and am sincere in my regret, chances are I'll be understood and even respected for my stand.

The art of assertion, or learning how to say no, is coming of age. Judy Amstutz, director of student personnel services at Loyola University Medical Center in Maywood, Illinois, and instructor at the College of Du Page near Chicago, teaches such a course in assertion training. She maintains that women have been trained to believe and to say, "I'm just a girl who can't say 'no,'" and that "women have been socialized always to please." She says, "One of the biggest parts of asserting yourself is knowing you have certain rights. You're the judge of your own behavior and no one else. You have the right to your own opinions and feelings."[3]

As usual, *Peanuts* character Lucy has something to say on this subject. "It's MY life, and I'll do whatever I want with it! I'm my own person! It's my life, and I'm the one who has to live it!!" After her tirade, she turns around and says sheepishly, "With a little help . . ."

The fast pace of life confuses me. Alvin Toffler points out in *Future Shock* that there's good reason for this, because there's less time for extended peaceful attention to one problem or situation at a time now. No wonder we "have a vague 'feeling' that things are moving faster." We face the "premature arrival" of tomorrow before we've caught our breath from today.[4]

A keen observer of our modern pace was quoted in a church bulletin (no name given): "This is the age of the half-read page, and the quick hash, and the mad dash; the bright night with the nerves tight, the plane hop with the brief stop; the lamp tan in a short span; the big shot in a good spot; the brain strain and the heart pain; the catnaps 'til the spring snaps—and the fun's all done."

I know that God never gives me more that I can do. And I realize the demands on my time as a wife, mother, and writer are meant to add dimensions to my life, not tear me apart. I often have to stop and ask myself, "Is this something the Lord has given me to do or is it of my own making?"

In my most panic-stricken moments, I often find myself in the absurd position of doing something I don't really care about. You'd think I was one of the last of the big-

The Gift of Time

time spenders. In *Please Don't Eat the Daisies,* Jean Kerr says that she suffered from similar problems because she's a compulsive reader. Of anything. She would read the labels on milk-of-magnesia bottles, enclosures with the monthly bills, or the yellow pages of the telephone directory. The only way she forced herself to get down to writing her book was to go out to the family car where she "froze to death or roasted, depending on the season." There was finally "nothing to do but write"—that is, after she'd tidied up the glove compartment.[5]

I become so intense, I forget to enjoy my work. I'm like the young man who moved from the city to the mountains and started to build his own cabin. One day as he was violently sawing a log, an old mountaineer came and watched him work. Like most city fellows, he worked as fast as he could to get the log sawed. "Now," the old man said, "when I saw, I just saws."

If I work through my day with my only aim as that of getting through in a hurry, I've lost a day in which to live to the fullest. That's what life is: one day at a time. The purpose of utilizing my time is not to take the joy out of living, but to put more into it.

I know better, but I forget. Some of my days are so frantic I'm reminded of the wall graffiti I heard about. One asks, "Is there intelligent life on earth?" Somebody had come along and added this postscript: "Yeah, but I'm only visiting."

Thoreau observed a long time ago that work was an expensive occupation because it took so much time from living. My work tends to expand and fill up all the time available, so I need to stay loose and reserve some uncommitted time in every day. Without the proper balance I operate like an alarm clock that's been wound too tight.

Whenever I feel myself suffering from what Ogden Nash called the "hardening of the oughteries," it's time to stop and reexamine my whole life plan, for something has gone wrong. Time is a gift to spend and enjoy like all my other gifts from God.

Am I learning something from it? If I save time but waste my life, what do I have? My son has a poster in his room that reminds me that the greatest use I can make of my life is to spend it for something that will outlast it. But what outlasts life? More life? And what about the time when life on earth will be ended?

I believe that this life is just the beginning. It's a learning experience, a testing ground, a prelude to eternity. Thus, I've always felt that as I grow older, my life should not be a time of winding down, but a winding up for graduation: a time for assessment, adjustment, and maybe even a bit of cramming for finals.

There are many books and articles on the use of time. But unless we know what it's all about, we're like the ants that Thoreau observed. Scurrying around and backtracking without any obvious purpose or progress may be the way for ants to live, but it is exhausting and fruitless and beneath the dignity of humans who are born in God's image.

Of all the advice that I've found useful from time-management experts, some suggestions have been invaluable to me:

Know where your time goes. According to Peter F. Drucker, author of *The Effective Executive,* most executives think they spend their time on the work they consider most important. He's found, however, that when they actually keep a record for several days, they usually discover it isn't that way at all. Knowing how you've used your time can help you manage that part of your time that can be brought under control.

So before you mount up and ride off in all directions, it pays to spend some time and actually write down how you spend your days. Then study your notes. Rather than "razzle-dazzle tactics," what's often needed is "right strategy." [6] Could some of your activities be done by someone else just as well or better? Could some of them be postponed to a later time with no harm done? What would happen if a few weren't done at all? If nothing would, don't do them.

Decide on your goals. When you don't have a goal, you can exhaust yourself by racing around but never cross the finish line. I've done that because I'm prone to jump into the thick of things before I know what my aim is. It's not lack of time that is my biggest enemy; it's sheer waste of it. And then it's not knowing what I want to do next.

As much as I protest in the process, this is what I do: I list my goals on a piece of paper in two columns, long-term and short-term. This helps to clarify them, and I can refer to the paper when I forget what I'm trying to do, which is often.

Just what are my goals in life? When the next six months is up, how would I like to have spent it? I try not to start with things I can't do anything about. I look for the major areas in which I can apply my best efforts and obtain outstanding results.

It seems ridiculous for me to be listing such ethereal ideas as, "I want to read all of the Great Books series" or "learn to speak French" when leftover egg is sticking to the breakfast plates and will have to be chipped off with a putty knife. But I go ahead and dream, knowing yesterday's unfulfilled dreams have a way of invading the subconscious and haunting my life later.

Then I place my goals in some order of importance. This isn't easy, but it has to be done. Would I rather have a clean kitchen floor or go out with my husband to see *Fiddler on the Roof*? Am I more interested in raising my own Big Boy tomatoes or watching my son march in the 4th of July parade? Would I rather sharpen up my lecture notes for my World Literature class or play a set of tennis? I want to be sure I'm spending my time on what's important to me.

"Making the right choices about how you'll use your time is more important than doing efficiently whatever job happens to be around," says Alan Lakein, author of *How to Get Control of Your Time and Your Life*.[7]

Now, for a plan of action. Make a weekly schedule that will represent all of your goals. On a blank sheet of paper draw seven lines down for each day of the week, and three large blocks across the sheet for morning, afternoon, and evening. Write down what you want to get done each day. It's important to consider which day and which hour is best for creative work and which for grocery shopping. Don't use prime time for mending socks! The plan needs updating and revising periodically to fit your changing needs and those of your family.

Now this is important: Each night before you go to bed, write down specifically what you're going to do the next day in the order of importance. By knowing what you're going to do first, you won't waste time and can get right to the task.

After completing the first thing on your list, you go on to the second and so on. An easy job will seem harder if you keep putting it off, so tackle that disagreeable job today as listed, instead of tomorrow. Then you'll have twenty-four hours to savor the feeling of having the job behind you. Do everything in the order in which you've written it until you have completed the list or the day is gone, whichever comes first. And don't be discouraged when you don't finish everything; start tomorrow's list with those left over from today.

Crowding a life, however, doesn't necessarily enrich it. Jess Lair doesn't try to do but a few important things each day. He says, "[That's the only way] I can get those crucial things done well and really be alive to what's going on around me the rest of the day. This way I don't need to throw days away because of being too busy." And when something important comes up, he can truthfully say, "I'm not busy." But part of it, he says, is that he doesn't "need being busy any more as a way to run away. He claims the beauty of it is that he gets a lot more and better work done now than he used to because he enjoys living.[8]

Don't overlook the waiting periods. Most people operate in the range of days and hours but waste their minutes. Their periods of waiting are used for that only and nothing more. Learn to be a wait-watcher. Never be in a doctor's office without something to do—a book to read, pen and paper for writing letters or making grocery lists. Some people keep a briefcase or strong shopping bag ready, a "waiting kit" of things they're working on in spare moments, whether at the office or at home.

Reserve time to recharge your battery. Woe is me when I forget this. It's something I never find time for—I have to make time. Sometimes when things are going well, I think I can cheat a little so I skimp on it. Pretty soon my whole life comes falling down around my ears, and I spend days wandering around in a fog of depression. Only after I've fought through the gray maze do I realize what's wrong: I've got a dead cell.

Any activity that fills my bucket should never be left to chance, so I put it in the schedule. It may involve being alone sometime during each day or week. Not many people understand my need for solitude. Most confuse aloneness with loneliness and frantically rush to fill up my hours. But certain springs can be tapped only when I'm alone. The artist has to be alone to create, and I must have some solitude to find again the true essence of my self, the real me. When I'm constantly with people, I tend to think and act in established patterns. It's as if I were programed with a limited number of alternatives as answers to my problems.

A walk in the park or baking a loaf of homemade bread may be just the touchstone I need. Someone once said, "Tell me what you do with yourself and what you think of when you're alone, and I'll tell you what you are."

Recently, I've come to pinpoint a need for close friends in the sense that Jess Lair calls "mutual need therapy."[9] I'm finding that some of my friends give me something I need; they lift me up. And yet many others with whom I associate are not good for me; they drain me. So I'm trying to change some of the people I see each week. Of course there are some people that I need to minister to, but I'm talking about what I need to recharge my battery.

Because time is such a precious gift, I can stand the waste of any other gift more than I can that of time. In the work I've done over the years in the business world, I've found many jobs that required periods of idleness. I found myself taking on more than I could possibly do to avoid those extremely tiring periods of idleness when I couldn't do work of my own but was required by some mysterious protocol to "look busy" or even worse, to "make work."

A lot of people spend approximately one-seventh of their lives on "Blue Monday" and another one-seventh on "Thank God, it's Friday." With such an attitude, they don't have to fear that life will come to an end, but rather that it won't have a beginning.

Every day is the day the Lord has made. How much better to be able to say about any tomorrow, "Thank God, it's morning." Not because the nights are so rough, but because the days are so great.

If I've really lived today, this day that God has given me, no moments will have been lost, and no important work undone. So, Lord, slow me down and help me to have that full and fascinating life you intend for me and all your children.

9.

The Gift of Relationships

I am not alone. I am one of God's children, and therefore I have relationships. Everybody I know is somebody to somebody. Or, as poet John Donne wrote, "No man is an island." There's a multiplicity of people wherever I go, and I react and interact with every person with whom I come in contact.

There is a classic example of this reaction chain: The wife gets up late because the alarm didn't go off and in her haste burns the toast. The disgruntled husband goes to the office and yells at his co-worker who thereupon returns home that night and quarrels with his wife. She screams at her son, who goes out and kicks the dog, who chases the cat.

Life isn't lived in a vacuum but in a whirlwind of people—before us, behind us, and to the sides. There are people where we are going, and people where we've been. They distract, interrupt, jostle, and crowd us as we're jammed into smaller and smaller areas. They're on the phone, in honking cars, and queuing up in supermarket checkout lines until we want to run home, lock the door, and go ARRGH!

More and more people feel the space invasion in their lives. Temple University's Center for the Study of Psychoeducational Processes conducted a workshop that taught participants space terms like *intimate space*—up to eighteen inches away from you—in which you can "almost feel body heat from the person next to you." *Personal space* is defined as one to four feet for most people; if you "step inside uninvited," they'll step back. The next zone, *social space*, is from four to twelve feet, or just far enough so you can focus on the entire body. *Public space* is that shared by others in an official capacity, like with your boss.[1]

Ethical questions are being raised today that Grandma would never have imagined. Who has the right to move through my personal space? Can space be owned by anyone? And where do my rights end and yours begin? Indeed, how can living with others have become such a problem?

"You know what your trouble is?" says Lucy to Charlie Brown. "The whole trouble with you is that you're you!" "Well, what in the world can I do about that?" says Charlie. "I don't pretend to be able to give advice," says Lucy. "I merely point out the trouble!"

At a time when we can communicate in living color with the moon, we seem most unable to communicate with those nearest to us. Could it be that our need to reach out farther and farther into outer space stems from an inner hunger to communicate with the people around us?

We care about the kids struggling with drug problems, the man down the street who has lost his job. But when we can't seem to make an effort to let them know, it comes off that we "don't give a rip." We have developed a kind of cultural conditioning that has convinced us we don't know enough to get involved in other people's lives. Their problems appear too complex for us. Our advanced technological age seems to tell us, "See a professional." Anyhow, it's best not to get involved when we're so incapable of dealing with our own anxieties.

Involvement in other people's lives can be quite painful. We often hide behind impersonal projects in the church because personal relationships are much more difficult to handle and much more costly to ourselves. It's less demanding to send money, for example, to a missionary than it is to meet the needs of a lonely widow across town.

"A ship in a harbor is safe," someone pointed out on a poster, "but that is not what ships are built for." Man was created for love relationships, and we must somehow learn how to love.

The concept of Christianity is never singular; it involves relationships, not just to God, but to each other. The idea of a person being a Christian in isolation isn't even considered in the Bible. Look at all the ways Jesus says to relate to others: pray for one another; love one another; exhort and encourage one another; comfort one another; rejoice with each other; bear each other's burdens; and submit to one another.

Bobbie Holley, in *Person to Person,* notes that "it's almost impossible for a person to have a real relationship with God until he has known a loving, fulfilling relationship with another person."[2] If we don't love our brother and sister whom we have seen, we can't love God whom we have not seen.

When Bennett Cerf was head of Random House, he once appeared on an NBC program called "Conversation" whose topic of the day was, "What are you most afraid of?" Different guests discussed matters of world importance, and they finally reached the consensus that it was annihilation from the bomb that they feared the most. Cerf had remained silent throughout most of the discussion, but when pressed, he admitted what he feared most was not being loved.

Anne Morrow Lindbergh, in *Locked Rooms and Open Doors*, differs with people who speak of love as if you gave it away "like an armful of flowers." She describes love as "a force in you that enables you to give *other* things. It is the motivating power. It enables you to give strength and power and freedom and peace to another person. It is not a result; it is a cause."[3]

Christians should be the best lovers in the world, yet many of our relationships are in a mess because we struggle with a lot of misconceptions about love. Rather, I believe we need to recognize the following characteristics of love:

Love is a feeling and a commitment. The source of love is God, for God is love. We love him because he first loved us. When I begin to understand a little of God's love—what he's done for me and continues to do for me—my response is a feeling of gratefulness that grows until I want to return that love, until I can't keep from it. It's my way of saying, "Lord, you're coming through loud and clear." So I ask him, "What would you have me do?" And then I commit myself to doing his will.

It's been my experience that just telling people they should love is not very helpful. It may make us feel guilty because we know we should, and so what do we do? We get very busy to overcome our feelings of guilt, and every time we pause for breath, we start feeling guilty all over again.

The romantic myth we have long accepted is that we "fall in love" with someone as if it were some sort of accidental, mysterious process beyond our control, and we confuse the feeling of physical attraction with love. Complicating things further is the fact that our feelings change from time to time, and relying on them as our sole guide damages love relationships.

So when the feeling is not there, the discipline of commitment allows me to hang on until the "warm fuzzies" return. When my husband and I have had a misunderstanding, I get pretty disgruntled with him, but my decision to be his life partner allows me to penetrate that feeling and say to myself, "Now, cool it, sis. I know this can be worked out."

When my older son's stereo causes my eyes to lock, and my younger son's quarters smell like a condemned locker room where the only thing left on a clothes hanger is a backpack, my feelings are about as dependable as an active volcano. But I remind myself, "These guys are only out on loan." When I discipline them, I don't feel very good inside, but I'm committed to helping them mature and learn things like responsibility. It's a decision I made before they were conceived.

Because of the confusion, we could say love is a decision, not a feeling. But I have come to the conclusion both feeling and commitment must be present. If an emotion remains only a feeling, it's love that died a-borning. Feeling is the beginning point, and a very vital one; without it there's only a "grit-your-teeth" kind of attitude which becomes more of a duty-work response than a love-grace response.

Love is unconditional and accepting. The book of Ephesians grounds all relationships in Christ: husbands and wives; parents and children; fellow Christians with each other; slaves and masters. Ideally, we react as we do because of the way Jesus acts toward us, and we reach out to others as he reaches out to us.

God didn't make any of the people in my life as I would have made them. Many seem weird and even ungodly, but I know he created every one in his own image. God didn't put them here to live up to my expectations. Indeed, what would I want them to be like? Me, I guess. But when I look at the mess I make of my life sometimes, how can I be upset by what they're doing? Who am I to throw rocks? Ralph Waldo Emerson advised us, "Never try to make anyone like yourself—you know, and God knows, that one of you is enough."

Catch-22 is that you can't change anyone even if you try, and it destroys the best of relationships. Yet I suppose there's not a person alive who never wanted to change someone, sometime.

I want to be able to be myself without your interference, but I'm not willing to let you be you. In essence, that says I don't want to let you be responsible to God for yourself. I want to make you over. You see, I've got this little plank in my own eye, but, brother, or sister, look at that terrible little splinter in yours! Working you over helps to take my mind off myself.

If I can't make you over, at least I want you to agree with me because that assures me I'm right. And if there's anything a law-keeping person wants, it's to be sure he's right.

Why do we get so shook up when everybody doesn't agree? Does living in peace and harmony require everyone to sing the same note? "That ain't harmony," says Wally Armbruster, in a little book called *A Bag of Noodles*. "That, baby, is monotony. Harmony happens when people sing different notes . . . and even some which sound (at first) like discord suddenly start to sound great . . . once your ear gets used to the idea."

David Viscott, instructor at the University of Boston Medical School, psychiatric consultant for the State of Massachusetts, and author of six books, described in a *Houston Chronicle* interview what he believed the goal in human relationships to be—a condition in which people "act as midwives to the other's best self—not take over the whole operation."[4]

When I give up playing God, that means giving up manipulation too. No human being that God has made has the right to manipulate another. God didn't give us relationships so that we could dominate and control. The current avalanche of books on wife/husband relationships, and even most of the books on leadership, advocate thinly disguised manipulation techniques that one can use to gain what one wants. Even if it's "for their own good" (and we always insist so), it is devastating to use people for one's own purposes. Sooner or later this will be apparent to the one who's being manipulated, and trust will be completely destroyed.

And we can forget about our relationships with others if we haven't been able to accept ourselves. We're in no shape to tackle anyone else. Acceptance means we accept our feelings and our needs, but not necessarily all of our behavior. We're trying to change that as we grow up.

Jess Lair says it this way in *I Ain't Well—But I Sure Am Better:* "Deep mutual relationships give me the strength to accept more people. They give me the calm and self-respect that helps me move more of my relationships out of dislike up to courtesy and respect. And from courtesy and respect into acceptance." He thinks most of us work this the other way. "Instead of spending lots of time loving the easy ones," he says, "we're struggling to love the hard ones," not realizing "it's best to start at the top and work down."[5]

Love listens. Anyone can talk, but only a true friend listens, and this doesn't mean just waiting until the other finishes so we can express ourselves. "The first duty of love," Paul Tillich said, "is to listen." But more than responding from a sense of duty, love *wants* to listen because that is how we love more.

I've been a parent and teacher for many years, and I've

found that tends to make me lose the art of listening. I'm so accustomed to the sweet sound of my own authoritative voice spouting forth golden words of wisdom. But when my teenager goes into his cave and turns on his stereo, that's my cue to do more listening. His loud, rhythmic music is saying something.

General George C. Marshall's formula for handling people was to listen to the other person's story; listen to the other person's full story; and listen to the other person's full story first.[6]

Love is sensitive to others. There's a touching story about a little girl who came home late from a friend's house. When her angry mother confronted her, she explained she was late because Sally broke her doll. "But that's no excuse. You couldn't fix it," the mother said. "But Mama, I just had to stay and help her cry." And in our love relationships, we often need to stay and help someone cry.[7]

Personally, I do a lot of crying. My family has grown accustomed to it. Tears, like laughter, I consider to be great catharsis. They not only clear my emotional highways but cleanse my contact lenses. I have a theory they even moisturize the areas around my eyes so they don't wrinkle so fast.

Love has to have spontaneity to exist. Whenever we have the urge to do something wildly warm and loving for someone, we tend to hesitate and ask what they might think. Mostly I have found people to be overjoyed once they recover from the initial shock.

For example, I've become an impulsive note-sender. Monthly bills and unanswered letters to my relatives pile up on my desk while I write to people I've never met except through the pages of their books or articles. Some of them even answer me, and one man even called me long-distance the other day in response to my letter to say, "Hey, I hear what you're saying out there. I love you too."

The Gift of Relationships

Recently, while rereading the story Jesus told in Luke 10:25–37, I pondered again why the Samaritan helped the injured man. Suddenly the words of verse 33 jumped out at me, "He felt compassion." Not hatred for this man who despised his whole race, and not even obligation, but simply compassion. Why? Had the Samaritan himself felt such a need in his life? Did he wonder if he might be the next victim? Or was he aware that he was already a kind of victim himself?

Someone once pointed out that when you extend your hand to me, you become my neighbor. And when I take your hand, I am your neighbor.

Love frees and liberates. No one ever knew less about love than I did when I first met the man who has been my husband now for almost twenty-four years. I believe God sent him to free me. I was such a stranger to myself, but he knew I needed someone to say, "It's okay to be you." He gave me both the courage to investigate and support whenever I failed.

Dietrich Bonhoeffer describes the kind of freedom he gave me in *Life Together:* "The freedom of the other person includes all that we mean by a person's nature, individuality, endowment. It also includes his weaknesses and oddities, which are such a trial to our patience, everything that produces frictions, conflicts, and collisions among us."[8]

Real love sees all people as free beings without labels, only as individuals whom God loves. Neither possessive nor pushy, this kind of liberation builds us up and releases us back to our own unique selves. As Bobbie Holley wrote, "I must bear you in your freedom and you must bear me in my freedom; that is, we must let each other be what we are."[9]

More than that, when I know I'm free, then I can be free inside.

Love heals and ministers. The best medicine for most of what ails the human creature is love, according to one wise physician who has been practicing medicine for over thirty years. When asked, "What if it doesn't work?" he says, "Why, then double the dose."

Healthy people walk around looking for someone to love, while emotionally disturbed people scream, "Love me, love me." Dr. Thomas P. Malone, an Atlanta psychiatrist, says that's what psychiatry is all about. "Almost every emotional problem can be summed up in one particular bit of behavior: it's a person walking around screaming, 'For God's sake, love me.' And he goes through a million different manipulations to get someone to love him." When you see changes in him, it's when he realizes that if he gives up screaming, "love me," and goes to the business of loving someone, then he can get all the love he's been screaming for all his life.[10]

Those who work with Alcoholics Anonymous and Emotions Anonymous, which is patterned after AA, say that people who desperately need help themselves can be very healing for others, because they recognize their need for each other. Their own needs and hurts are the very thing that help them heal others. "To ease another's heartache," Abraham Lincoln once said, "is to forget one's own."

Touching is important in ministering to one another. We seem to long to be close to other people and to want to show it by hugging and squeezing and patting and crying on each other's shoulders.

Our Puritan heritage leads us to think of all bodily contact as sensual, but Jesus often touched those whom he healed, and touching plays an important part in giving encouragement, expressing tenderness, and showing emotional support. Our own inadequate feelings and misunderstandings about our body have created these invisible barriers.

In one of her columns, Dr. Joyce Brothers made the statement that in every mental institution one finds a number of patients who refuse or are afraid to be touched. This fact may indicate that people who are free to admit their need to be cuddled and loved are usually better adjusted and find it easier to go out and face the world than those who are not.

Love takes time. Some authorities say the average American moves about fourteen times in his lifetime, and that one-fifth of the people change addresses at least once a year, making the U-Haul van as familiar as the garbage truck. According to Alvin Toffler, the average residence in one place in most major U.S. cities is less than four years.[11]

In the twenty years or so my husband has been a minister, we have lived in five cities in Texas, three other states, and one foreign country, not to mention a few places that were little more than wide spots in the middle of a farm-to-market road. Including the times we've returned to college for advanced work, we've made at least ten major moves. At times I despair of ever decorating anything but the car. But like all the other millions of people in the same boat, we must somehow slow down the flow-through of people in our life.

Forced to become proficient in the "hurry-up welcome," more and more we turn to temporary and interpersonal relationships where there's little time or commitment involved. The greater the mobility of a person, the more brief, temporary face-to-face encounters he has. Our commitment to our relationships appears to correlate with their duration. As Toffler explains, "we have all learned to invest with emotional content those relationships that appear to us to be 'permanent' and relatively long-lasting, while withholding emotion, as much as possible, from short-term relationships."[12]

French sociologist Alain Touraine thinks people move so much because "having already made one change and being less attached to the community, they are readier to move again. . . ."[13] Knowing that no move is final, that you'll again gather up your belongings and migrate, you figure, "What's the use?"

Unable to become deeply involved with everyone we meet in urban America, where it's less possible to know our neighbors intimately than in the small communities of yesteryear, we maintain superficial and partial contact with a few. We move away from what Martin Buber calls "I-thou" relationships of respect and reverence and concern, and fall into "I-it" relationships in which we regard people as objects. As long as we don't become involved with them, we can define them merely in functional terms: she's my hairdresser; he's my barber; she's my secretary. We become interested only in the efficiency of the druggist to fill our prescription for Librium and the mechanic to put on our Midas muffler. We don't care whether he's an alcoholic or that his son-in-law is a paraplegic. This "modular man," as Toffler calls him, could be interchanged with any other one who can perform the same service. God forbid! We can now add one more creation to our "throw-away society": the disposable man.

Love is being real. "Man, that's for real," is an expression going around these days. Phoniness is out and genuineness is in.

My friend and teacher Dr. Donald C. Stewart, author of *The Authentic Voice,* likes the word *authenticity.* He relates it to "self-discovery" and thinks of it as "a process of acquiring both a more objective and a psychologically deeper sense of the person you are. It is a kind of revelation in which you not only begin to see yourself through the eyes of others, but acquire a fundamental sense of individuality beyond the complex of roles you play in life."

It's the process of finding out what you really believe instead of what you thought you believed, says Dr. Stewart.

The Gift of Relationships

Once you learn to ask the right questions of yourself and acquire the wisdom and courage to give honest answers, you're on your way to speaking with an authentic voice.[14]

What does it mean to be real with others? I don't think I even remotely understood what it meant until I read Jess Lair's books. About his first book, *I Ain't Much Baby— But I'm All I've Got,* he says, "Originally I was going to call this book *Real Is Love* because I don't know of anything I have ever seen that is more loving that one person can do for another than to tell that other person how it is really with them in their deepest heart. To give, in a sense, a part of yourself." [15]

We confirm our own reality by sharing it with others. Each real relationship that we manage enables us to reach out more and more to others, to deeper and richer relationships, and eventually move from the easy ones to the hard ones.

To discover the real person, that authentic self we talked about in chapter one, is further complicated by the images reflected back to us from countless persons around us. Oliver Wendell Holmes said there were six persons always present when two persons enter into a conversation: X as X thinks he is, X as Y thinks he is, and X as God knows he is. Then there's Y as Y thinks he is, Y as X thinks he is, and Y as God knows Y is.[16]

The person that God knows me to be is the one in touch with reality, the one that's open to the special plan God has for me.

How do I recognize if I'm being real with people? When they're real back with me. And when it's not working, Jess Lair notes, it's when I'm not being very real, because the more real I am, the more real people there are around me.

John Powell, author of *Why Am I Afraid To Tell You Who*

I Am?, cautions us, however, against thinking of ourselves as static and formed realities. "There is no fixed, true and real person inside of you or me, precisely because being a person necessarily implies becoming a person, being in process." The things that define my person are: what I "think, judge, feel, value, honor, esteem, love, hate, fear, desire, hope for, believe in, and am committed to."[17] Searching for realness, then, becomes a way of life, not a destination.

Love also receives. Givers who cannot take in return miss out too. While it's more blessed to give than receive, love is like the quality of mercy that blesses both him that gives and him that takes. When I receive spontaneous gifts from you with graciousness, I enhance your sense of worth and our relationship grows.

Love in the New Testament is always described in action. It's something we do. Ah, but it's much easier to substitute discussion for doing, to debate and ponder endlessly the practice of these realities rather than put them into practice. We can sing the words to the song, "They'll know we are Christians by our love," but they're only words until we do something.

We choose few if any of the people with whom we daily come into contact and probably think of them as being accidental to our lives. But they are relationships God has given us. The cranky co-worker, the pompous boss, the loud-mouthed kid across the street may be the irritants through whom God helps us to grow. In fact, one of the areas of life in which I feel we can really measure just how much we're growing is that of relationships. Here's where the daily battles are being fought. Corrie ten Boom, in *The Hiding Place*, assures us: "Every experience God gives us, every person is the perfect preparation for the future that only He can see."[18]

10.

The Gift of Marriage

When the Lord God said, "It isn't good for man to be alone," the first marriage relationship began, and without a doubt the first marital problems too. After Adam and Eve disobeyed God and were driven from the garden, that beautiful relationship between the first couple and God, and between each other, was forever changed. But God has been working out his plan to heal the broken ties ever since.

Of all the gifts God has given us, this one—marriage—must be handled with the most care because it is the closest of all relationships. The battle between the sexes may be the only war in town, but it's often the hottest because the second hardest thing in all the world must be to live with another person. The hardest is to live alone.

The Jewish term for marriage, *kiddushin*, comes from a

root word meaning "holy." Since holiness is related to wholeness in Jewish thought, the union of husband and wife both sanctifies marriage and indicates a situation in which both parts make up the whole.

Sometimes I hesitate to put my thoughts into print for everyone to "tsk, tsk" over and pick apart my inconsistencies. This is especially risky with respect to such a fragile thing as the marriage relationship, formed as it is between frail human beings who have feet of clay. But I had more than the normal sense of doom about this chapter when I read in the newspaper the other day about a couple who wrote a book called *Living Together,* but who admitted they had to finish it after they had separated. "Now we wonder," the wife said, "whether we'll be able to use what we know to stay together." I'm grateful this is just a chapter, not a whole book.

My husband, Robert, and I will celebrate our twenty-fourth anniversary next spring. Looking back over our years together, we came to the conclusion that when two out of four marriages end in divorce in the United States, we must have something pretty special. And though it wasn't really clear to us in the beginning, we believe that God brought us together, and because we've trusted him and looked to him for direction, he has given us a good life together.

Robert and I met in church, of all places—not that it was such a strange place for me to be, but Robert had been an atheist up to a few weeks before. And he was, of all things, "a nice young man" my mother wanted me to meet. Three months later we were married.

Our sons have often asked me what was different about their father. I think it was that he saw me as a person and gave me the greatest compliment I'd ever received when he asked me what I thought about something.

Looking back on it now, I realize he wasn't the only

The Gift of Marriage

man in the world for me, that I believe more nearly what Jim Reynolds says in *Secrets of Eden: God and Human Sexuality:* "Marriage involves finding a right person, but it is not contingent upon finding *the* right person. . . . The biblical emphasis focuses on a person becoming a right person and with God's help committing oneself to another right person."

I am not given to boasting, and I have a great deal of concern and compassion for those who have known nothing but hell-on-earth marriages. But I also want to emphasize that marriage takes work. We got to the "top" the hard way—fighting our own laziness and ignorance every step. VISTA'S slogan fits every relationship I've ever known, including marriage relationships: "If you're not part of the solution, then you're part of the problem."

"Tentative suggestions" is the heading I wanted to give these next few comments. However, I believe each marriage is as unique as the individuals themselves, and so, rather than advise or suggest anything, I decided on the title "Some of the Things I Think We May Do Right." (This also gives me more breathing space.)

We quit looking around. It's a troublesome habit to break if you've been doing it for ten or twelve years. I told myself, "What I have will do," and other men ceased to exist as other than friends. Robert and I never actually said to each other, "Hey, honey, I quit looking," but complete trust existed between us from the beginning because our moments together were so reassuring.

People have occasionally asked me, "Aren't you jealous of all those women who're always seeking counsel from your husband?" I can honestly say no. Certainly I realize he's felt physical attraction for other women, but I'm confident he has the discipline to keep it just that as long as our own relationship is good.

I've never been able to imagine myself married to anyone

but Robert Humphries, and I have never found any man I wish I'd married instead of him. (The other men I've known aren't all that bad—but he's that good!) And besides, I've got all this time invested in our relationship now.

We agree on the boss in the family. The Lord is the master and head of our home; at least we've always aimed for that, and we don't need another one.

Decisions that have to be made and things that need to be done are discussed by both of us, and we try to determine what is best for everyone concerned. In areas where one of us has more knowledge, ability, and experience, we rely on that person's best judgment, and if one of us feels especially strong about an issue, that influences the decision. Any other method would be not only ridiculous but foolish. We have both erred enough in our judgments to realize that we need all the help we can get, that two heads really are better than one.

There has never been a problem in our marriage in this area, and we can't imagine any in the future. In spite of all the talk, past and present, about how a home must have order and therefore a leader, our partnership has not threatened our relationship but given it greater meaning.

But what about the biblical admonition of dominance and submission? As expressed more fully in chapter 5, "The Gift of Sexuality," I do not believe the Lord ever intended for twentieth-century marriage relationships to maintain the same sort of hierarchy of dominance and submission that prevailed historically during biblical times any more than I believe he intended slavery and racial injustice to continue. If he did, consistency would demand that a woman return to the obviously inferior position she held during the first century.

Jesus came to liberate men and women from their sins,

The Gift of Marriage

including the sins of inhuman domination over each other. He came to earth, as a human, to show both men and women the way: submission to the Lord and to each other. The message of the New Testament is one of mutual consideration, submission for everyone, and dominance by none.

Much of the confusion today is due to the interpretation of statements by Paul, not Jesus. Paul himself says this about his teaching: "And I, brethren, could not speak to you as to spiritual men, but as to men of flesh, as to babes in Christ. I gave you milk to drink, not solid food; for you were not yet able to receive it. Indeed, even now you are not yet able" (1 Cor. 3:1, 2). In context, Paul is trying to lead to maturity a group of people who had all kinds of problems—including the continuation of the covenant of circumcision, eating meat sacrificed to idols, and the customs of hair lengths and praying and prophesying with the head uncovered as being symbols of authority. Indeed it's often hard to determine the eternal principles from the temporary measures and still be in harmony with the rest of the New Testament teaching. While I don't presume to know all the answers to the male/female relationship, I see more and more evidence of what it is *not*.

Books on the relationship between Christian men and women have rolled off the press at an unprecedented rate, says Virginia Mollenkott, and instead of helping, they have further confused the picture because they tend to dehumanize marriage by laying "the burden of marital success solely on the shoulders of the woman, requiring all the psychological adjustments of her and blaming only her if success is not achieved. In the process, the husband is often raised to the level of an absolute norm, as if he were God, while the wife is nullified into the worst kind of self-sacrificing idolatry."[1]

Dr. Mollenkott quotes one writer who insists that such

female submission be done without "resentment or open hostility, pussy cat manipulation, and power-plays, either overt or subtle." I agree with Dr. Mollenkott that it is indeed hard to say who is damaged more, the husband who allows himself to be worshiped, or "the woman who places her all on the altar of her husband's approval." The growth of both partners is stunted by such attitudes.

Many of the current writers imply that the development of a woman's personal potential is secondary to the husband's development. Such bad advice ultimately produces unhealthy relationships for everyone.

The Bible presents the ideal situation as one in which the submission by one person is regarded so lovingly by the other that he or she returns the same Christlike submission. But submission becomes only a manipulative tool when it includes flattering insincerity, self-deception, and thinly veiled contempt for the other person's ego. When I showed some of these books to my husband, he was both shocked and disgusted that such advice is being presented as biblical and Christlike!

Such teaching has invited men to dominate women with a heady sense of power and pride, but an equally harmful result is in its encouragement for women to bury or hide their gifts from God and lead immature, irresponsible, and passive lives. And when a woman believes that the only way she can relate to God is through the authority of her husband, I fear she may never be able to stand alone before Him as a mature, responsible person.

On the other hand, I thank God for such books like *All We're Meant to Be* by Letha Scanzoni and Nancy Hardesty. I found this book only after I had wandered and searched through most of the same territory on my own. My copy is splotched with the tears of joy I shed when I discovered I was not alone, a knowledge that was important in the

The Gift of Marriage

healing process which had to take place before my growth could continue.

No one has to dominate or control the other in a healthy relationship, not when both submit to Christ and to each other. Either one may be the spokesman for the couple at various times, just as in a democratic society an elected official may speak for the people who appoint him.

Whatever the beliefs of those around us, my husband and I have based our relationship on mutuality. We have tried to find ways to minister to each other, acknowledging that sometimes his needs have been more pressing, and at other times, mine have been. Other Christian couples we know also have beautiful, healthy, growing relationships between human beings who are equal as people but whose roles and sexuality are different. To them, as to us, this subject presents no barriers, and I thank God the number is growing.

We maintain our separate identities. A marriage relationship should be one in which two people are willing to be themselves, regardless of the sacred cows that exist, and not what society or the church happens to define as maleness and femaleness. This is doubly hard when we live in a world where we are made to believe we are what we do.

One partner is always in danger of trying to be the one he thinks the other wants him to be instead of developing his own character. Playing roles that don't fit us does all sorts of strange things to our identity: He plays being masculine and she plays being feminine. He plays the kind of man he thinks the kind of woman she's playing ought to admire. She plays the kind of woman that she thinks the kind of man he's playing ought to desire.

If I'm not just an extension of my husband, and he's not just an extension of me, who are we? Whoever I am, I'm a woman, and I have to serve God as a woman.

Dr. Joyce Brothers, in *The Brothers System for Liberated Love and Marriage*, admits that it's not easy for a woman to come by a clear understanding of her true role, especially in the early days of her marriage. Pressured by society, she tends to subordinate herself and her interests to those of her husband, and love makes this easy. Most men say they aren't as upset over this arrangement as their wives. As one man put it, "Why should I be, when it so clearly caters to me and my whims?" It takes a very wise and loving man to admit, even to himself, that some of his happiness may be gained at the sacrifice of his wife's.[2]

Failure to maintain separate identities often causes relationships to develop into one-way affairs, with the bored wife waiting for the husband to come home and make her feel alive. In this situation, years of marriage can narrow her interests to new ground-meat recipes and her children's Little League or Campfire activities.

Henri Nouwen, associate professor in pastoral theology at Yale Divinity School, pointed out in an article that "people can only be together when they affirm each other as separate human beings who receive their sense of self not from each other but from God." He further said, "When husband and wife expect from each other the fulfillment of their deepest need, they put inhuman claims on each other and develop a suffocating relationship."[3]

No one should be so immersed in another human being—husband, wife, lover, parent, or child—that the precious self God created is devalued. And if one mate can help the other to value him or herself, to feel loved and secure, he or she can reclaim precious personhood. This means not just accepting but also supporting each other's identity.

Gabrielle Burton, in *I'm Running Away From Home But I'm Not Allowed To Cross The Street*, speaks of the problem of women who exist only for other people only to find

The Gift of Marriage

that when they're gone, they have no more reason for being. "In some cases, they are nothing, for when one depends totally upon a relationship for her identity, a cessation or altering of that relationship can cease the identity."[4]

Anne Morrow Lindbergh, in *Gift from the Sea*, refers to the best relationship as one that is "not a limited, mutually exclusive one . . . and not a functional, dependent one . . . but the meeting of two whole fully developed people as persons."[5]

Real love is not total absorption in each other, but it looks outward in the same direction together. Love multiplies joys and divides griefs. It makes burdens lighter. It makes us stronger so we can reach out and become involved with life in ways we dare not risk alone.

I like what Kahlil Gibran recommends in *The Prophet:* "And let there be spaces in your togetherness, and let the winds of the heavens dance between you. . . . And stand together yet not too near together: For the pillars of the temple stand apart, and the oak tree and the cypress grow not in each other's shadow."[6]

We believe marriage is a becoming process. Unlike the fairy tale—boy meets girl, they fall in love, and they live happily ever after—Genesis 2:24 suggests much more is involved: ". . . And they shall become one flesh." Two people completely becoming one in all areas of their lives doesn't happen at the altar or on a honeymoon but through growth on the part of each partner. It takes a life of discovering each other.

. . . as well as a growing-up process. Childhood for many is a blissful time of play and fantasy during which one is permitted to be utterly selfish and narcissistic, all the while being tenderly loved and given delightful gifts without being expected to give anything in return.

Do most women more or less consciously want to remain

children all their lives? Clare Booth Luce believes so, according to a letter to her niece printed in the *Bulletin* of the Baldwin School and condensed in *Reader's Digest.* She insisted that all human beings, male or female, subconsciously desire to remain children, but that it is easier for a woman to remain a child in a country where the high standard of living makes it possible for a man to afford a child-wife. The image of the average American housewife has historically and traditionally been a child-wife who is "happily playing house, married to an adoring husband whose harshest criticism of her is that she isn't giving him the right brand of coffee or getting out the ring around his collar." Media commercials confirm that such a girl-child sex object has bouncy hair, inviting lips, and a heavenly smelling body. Obviously she is intended by nature to receive endless goodies and gifts from her husband-lover.[7] Such a husband-lover may appear eager at first to play the grown-up role of father-protector to his child-wife; later he may subconsciously want to be the happy, selfish, waited-upon child himself and his wife to be the loving mommy.

What a healthy relationship this spawns! Each wanting to play the child while desiring the other to play the parent—all the while hollering for the other to "grow up, for heaven's sake." This verifies what I have long suspected: that marriage is often a promise between children living in a house called man's castle but resembling a nursery.

Mrs. Luce's assessment parallels that which I have very often observed to be true. But if human beings do subconsciously want to remain children, this wish points to a weakness that should be overcome. We are not supposed to keep on being children but are supposed to grow up. Thus it is especially alarming to read some of the recent best sellers aimed at Christians.

The Gift of Marriage

Dr. William Freeman, associate professor of speech communications at California State University, speaking to the Speech Communication Association in Houston, presented a paper called "A Primer for Submissive/Machiavellian Rhetoric: Helen Andelin's *Fascinating Womanhood.*" He referred to the book as comical, ridiculous, and silly, but sinister and manipulative. But the most distressing thing about the book, he said, is that "it can work."

Ms. Andelin holds up a character from Charles Dickens's *David Copperfield,* pointing out Dora's "childlike, trusting" ways. "At times she would shake her curls as little girls do." By watching the antics of little children, we too can learn to stamp our feet and shake our curls and pout and get "adorably angry" at ourselves. But Ms. Andelin counsels that our "spunk must be mostly pretense."[8] In my opinion, it is poor advice to recommend such cuteness and dishonesty to women who are trying to become more like Christ. A woman is what is supposed to happen to a little girl.

We are committed to each other. Our marriage has priority over the children, work, our parents, and our friends. Our sons say the most reassuring knowledge they have is that we love each other most in all the world, even above them.

Elton Trueblood expresses the idea in *The Common Ventures of Life* that marriage is not a contract, since the conditions often change, but a commitment, and a religious one at that. A contract assumes we have certain obligations to meet and rights to expect. The right to happiness seems guaranteed by our constitution, and so when one of the partners fails to receive this right, he feels justified in terminating the contract. Because the other has failed to deliver happiness to him.

We know the beauty of a good sex life. I'm reminded of the comment I once read in *Reader's Digest* about a boys' school in England that merged with a girls' school: "There are some things boys can do that girls cannot, and some things that girls can do that boys cannot. But believe me, the best are the things that boys and girls can do together."

Two polemic attitudes generally seem to exist about the gift of sex. One indicates the belief that it's a strictly biological function to be used selfishly; the other shows a reverence for God's gift to be celebrated in ways that bring genuine joy to each partner.

I cannot be compartmentalized. If my body is to be a living sacrifice to God, and if God said after making his creation, that "it was very good," that means all of me. "Just as love has its compassionate moments," my friend Jim Reynolds says in *Secrets of Eden: God and Human Sexuality,* "it also has its passionate moments."

A man and wife can have deep spiritual moments during which their sexual embrace adequately communicates their love. It's the ultimate spontaneous response between two individuals who regard each other as persons to minister to, not objects to be used. But when there are unresolved conflicts, they show up in bed. Thus, generally, as our spiritual life goes, so goes our sex life.

"The married man or woman," Jim Reynolds further says, "who prizes prayer, but who does not hope to experience God in sexual passion needs not praise but Christian therapy. He or she should not be described as spiritual but rather as disembodied."[9]

Rollo May, psychologist and author of *Love and Will,* complained that our society "has shifted from acting as though sex didn't exist at all to being obsessed with it, . . . and that we might seem, to a visitor from Mars dropping into Times Square, to have no other topic of communication."[10] Indeed, sex has become the solution for all of the world's problems. It's as if we expect love to grow out of sex, instead of love growing into sex.

Jess Lair, in *I Ain't Well—But I Sure Am Better,* compares

The Gift of Marriage

our obsession with sex to drinking water which is free and readily available. We're only conscious of thirst when we're thirsty and can't get any water, but as soon as we drink a few glasses, the thirst goes away and it's forgotten. The starving man, however, constantly thinks of food, and the thirsty man constantly thinks of drinking water. People wouldn't be so sex-starved if their deep emotional needs as well as their physical needs were being met in a manner sufficient to satisfy them. The person who has a successful sexual relationship doesn't need to go around bragging about how great it is, Jess points out, because he doesn't need to. He just smiles.[11]

Questions we've been asked about our marriage relationship:

Who brings home the bacon? One of the things that has come out of the liberation movement has been the right of a woman to go out and make a living on the same basis as a man, and that's as it should be.

Robert's profession was the one we concentrated on in the beginning, because of the times or because it was the right thing to do, I really don't know. And he's been the one who has mostly worked outside the home while I've mostly worked inside. But he's tried to give me the opportunity to catch up by encouraging me to do my thing. He knows I'd never be happy not being able to do something concrete beyond my immediate surroundings.

I've held eight-to-five jobs on numerous occasions, and while there was always a certain satisfaction, there was a real drain on my spirituality. It surely made me appreciate my husband. When he opened the door in the evening, my prime concern wasn't his lateness or that he didn't stop by the store for milk, but that he made it home at all.

I believe every person must have the freedom to do the kind of work each one wants to do, one that uses gifts as fully as possible. No one is liberated until both husband and wife are allowed to do that. A husband can be the breadwinner and the wife the homemaker and both be their real selves—but only if they're secure people doing what they're doing by choice.

We still have unresolved problems, but we're working on them. We are both products of our culture to some extent whether we like it or not. Intellectually, we may believe one way, but our feelings are often a mixed bag.

Norman M. Lobsenz interviewed scores of couples and reported his findings in *Woman's Day*. He concluded his article, "How Husbands Really Feel About Working Wives," with these words: "Despite their reservations and mixed feelings, most of today's husbands would not want to be married to Alice-sit-by-the-fire. They like the idea of a wife who can be self-reliant, who broadens her interest and skills, who shares family responsibilities, who is better able to understand what men must cope with on the job. . . . In short, for all their ambivalence, they prefer a woman who is clearly more of a partner in life. One husband summed it up this way: 'Which of us would want a wife who sat at home and waited for us to bring the world to her?' " [12]

Who handles the money? We've never had an arrangement of my money and your money—it's been our money. No matter who brought the check in, we both worked for it. The family budget is likewise agreed on by both of us. Because of my business background, I kept the books for the first number of years, but Robert says he likes to spend money more than I do so he does the check-writing now. He says it makes him more aware of our finances, and he isn't so prone to go out and buy something he doesn't need.

And do we ever disagree on how the money is to be spent? Of course! I doubt that any two people could ever agree exactly on this. But we both make the money, whether I work at home or away from home, and it's for both of us to decide how the money is to be spent. We are both stewards of the family bank balance.

Is your husband everything you expected? No, he isn't, but neither am I. No one could be that handsome, smart, kind, and funny. He's nothing like that, but I'll take him anyhow. There have always been surprises because we're both changing daily. The mathematical probabilities of that keep life interesting.

Walter Trobisch, in *Love Is A Feeling To Be Learned*, says, when comparing Sylvia's dream image of a future husband to the real thing: "She had learned the first lesson in love: one has to give up dreams, because they stand in the way of happiness." [13]

Love isn't enough to make a marriage. It won't succeed without it, but there's more to it. It means growing up, facing realities, and giving up childish ways.

Any quarrels? Plenty. Enough to keep us from becoming complacent about our relationship. There have been years when we seemed to have very few quarrels, and other times when we've had a great many. There seems to be a definite correlation between our periods of personal growth and our inability to live peacefully.

When one or the other of us is reaching out and trying to grow, that's when the most adjustments and the most misunderstandings seem to occur. And if you could see us on days when both of us are outgrowing our old skins and aren't yet comfortable in our new ones, you might wonder why I thought our relationship was something to write about. On those days, *I* wonder why I thought so!

But we always trust that, given enough time, we can work our problems out. We always have. Problems are inevitable in every relationship. What's important is to have ways to solve them and have a relationship that can hold up under conflicts.

Love is for growth as well as for pruning. There have been times when I've thought, "Lord, about this man *you* gave me—" But in my calmer moments, I've realized I've grown because of his inadequacies, and he's grown because of mine. Our failures are not his or mine, but ours—in communicating, in neglecting to exercise loving care, and in seeing to one another's needs.

Now that we're entering the midlife panic years and coming to grips with the gap between our dreams and our accomplishments, we realize we haven't had much success as the world counts it. Most everyone we know has a better job, a nicer home, old-age security, and money in the bank. But our life together has been our success, and our love holds us together and strengthens us for the hazards of life in which "everyone hurts somebody some time."

Once when my husband was away on an overnight trip, our son came into the bedroom and stretched out on the bed beside me.

"I expect this queen-size bed seems pretty big when Dad's gone," he said.

"The world's too big when he's gone," I said. And that's how I feel about my husband. It's not good for this woman to live alone.

It's a chilly world with just me. I can go through life without him, but having Robert to share with makes a lot of difference. I can smile, but we can laugh out loud. I can weep, but we can cry on each other's shoulder. I can dream, but we can build a utopia. I can grow older, but we can become nearer and dearer to each other.

The closest thing Robert came to making me a wedding promise was when he said, "I don't know what kind of life we'll have together, but I can promise you this. You'll aways have a tent to live in at least."

Then some ten years later, when things were looking up, he said, "Someday we'll be rich, honey."

Now after twenty-four years together, I finally know: We *are* rich. Someday we might even have some money.

Anne Morrow Lindbergh, in *Gift from the Sea,* sums it up for me: "Security in a relationship lies neither in looking back to what it was in nostalgia, nor forward to what it might be in dread or anticipation, but living in the present relationship and accepting it as it is now."[14]

11.

The Gift of Children

Before our children were born, our favorite expression was, "No child of ours will ever do such and such." But with the patter of tiny feet are 40 million words to eat. Like many other people, I knew a whole lot more about rearing children before I had some. The principles I believed in have remained about the same; it's just that whenever the heat of battle is upon me, I've found that knowing what should be done and being able to do it are two quite different things.

In *You Can Be a Great Parent,* Charlie Shedd said he had similar parent pains: "So today I seldom speak on parenthood. And whenever I do, after one or two old jokes, you'd catch this uncertain sound . . . 'Anyone here got a few words of wisdom?' " [1]

The Gift of Children

So you out there, if you know anything for sure, for God's sake, pass it on! It's too late to help me much, but the world needs it.

My husband and I have always believed in planned parenthood. Whether because we were aware of the population explosion and concerned with feeding a hungry world, or because we just wanted to avoid having so many kids who'd have to grow up like Topsy, I don't know. But we chose to bring children into the world, and like most parents-to-be, we had confidence we'd do a good job. We loved each other, and we had all of the tools of a Mental Health age, including a smattering of Dr. Spock.

I hadn't read *Please Don't Eat the Daisies* yet, but Jean Kerr took the words right out of my mouth shortly after our first baby was born: "Now the thing about having a baby—and I can't be the first person to have noticed this—is that thereafter you *have* it, and it's years before you can distract it from an elemental need by saying, 'Oh, for heaven's sake, go look at television.' " [2]

But we recovered from the initial shock and were enchanted enough with parenthood to plan another bundle of joy. We thought we were wisely spacing our children almost four years apart so their position as oldest and youngest child wouldn't cause personality damage. Not only that, the mistakes we'd made with the first could be corrected with the second. At least that's what we said, though I suspect that was more to keep from causing parent damage. And as for the mistakes, I fear it only permitted us to make exactly the opposite mistakes with the younger one.

Somewhere since that pristine beginning and the long summer during which the kids complained there was absolutely nothing to do and then sat and read Captain Marvel as we drove through Rocky Mountain National Park, things got confused. I felt the same way one frazzled father confessed: "I've wanted to run away from home more often since I've had kids than when I was a kid."

Parenting is often like rolling the rock of Sisyphus in Greek mythology. It's an endless, perplexing task. Yet most of us recognize a good parent when we see one, and in rare periods of calm, we even sense how to be one. But we don't seem to be able to do it.

Child psychology is big business these days. I've been reading books and articles since long before my children were born. Child experts remind us of hundreds of little, important things. For example, use pleasant requests instead of scoldings. Say, "You will need to pick up your toys in ten minutes," not, "Get that cotton-picking junk out of here, *right now.*"

Everyone knows that praise does wonders for the sense of hearing. I really believe in suggestions like Lorraine Collins made in *What's a Place Like This Doing to a Nice Girl Like Me?* She says a surefire system for getting a child to clean up his room without nagging is to find something positive you can say about it. Say, for instance, "You certainly do keep a neat ceiling!" [3]

I recognize the wisdom of such advice, but I could never seem to remember it when I needed it. I was too busy thinking I could make a fortune if I could invent a chocolate breakfast food that drains energy from kids.

Some of the information in these collections of advice, however, is pure hogwash. Remember when the current theory was to set a three- or four-hour feeding schedule for your new baby and teach him to adhere to it by letting him cry it out? If he filled his tummy with air and got the colic (a malady which also didn't exist), that would serve him right. He couldn't possibly be hungry more often; the book said so. And then there was the permissive stage when you were never supposed to deny your darling

The Gift of Children

anything he wanted because it would warp his personality.

Long ago I came to the conclusion that the first rule was to use your common sense. And so I came to regard any pure theory of child-rearing like the recipe for Granny's buttermilk biscuits. I couldn't possibly write it down. It's more a pinch of this and a dash of that. Then you pat 'em out like so, dab 'em in warm grease, and pop 'em in the oven. And then you just wait a spell 'til you see how they turn out.

My approach to parenting is now much like the one Dr. Samuel Johnson's blind housekeeper used when she poured tea. She put her finger inside the cup. I think the Air Force calls it "flying by the seat of your pants."

After watching our children's grandparents, I decided if we'd had grandchildren first, we might have done a better job.

While parents turn gray, grandparents celebrate, and it's their gaiety, plus lavishing of love and lollipops that make them so popular with the kids. They never arrive without an armful of goodies, are never too busy to read a Dr. Seuss book, or too broke to buy ten chances on a pony. And they hardly ever have to say no. They walk with a spring in their step, look ever so rested and chipper, and have all the patience in the world. They're parents who are having a grand time because their children are already grown.

So, how do we get from the Pablum to the whoopee stage? More specifically, what sustains us through the years of looking for dual-purpose baby food that serves as a floor wax and out of the dog days of how-long-Lord-how-long?

Babies don't come equipped with instructions pinned to their pink, wrinkled *derrières*. I always thought the Bible must be filled with instructions because my mother used to quote "Children, obey your parents" so much. But most of it is rather general, like "Train up a child in the way he should go." And yet everyone, including God, seems to think we ought to know how to do the job.

Maybe we indeed do have a script. Not laid out in black and white, but running between Genesis and Revelation is a rough draft of "how our Heavenly Father parents us without patronizing us."

Our Father knows how to love. "See how great a love the Father has bestowed on us, that we should be called children of God; and such we are," 1 John 3:1 tells us. He loved us long before the foundation of the world. His very name is synonymous with love; he is love. He knows that we need love, especially when we don't deserve it, and he continues to love us, no matter what. However naughty we've been, or whatever monstrous sins we have committed, his arms are always open to us. His response is always the most loving response possible.

This is *agape* love, which Bobbie Holley describes in *Person to Person* as "love that asks nothing in return, love that goes out to the unlovely and unappreciative, love that confirms people and sees in them what they can become, love that goes beyond all reason, love that is impractical and extravagant, love that pours out costly ointment and washes feet, love that accomplishes the impossible, forgives the deepest hurts and is finally crucified if necessary." [4]

It's the kind of love described in an old short story she tells in which a small boy is bewitched into murdering his mother. He takes the heart from her lifeless body to a witch who lives up on the hill, but he stumbles along the rugged path and drops the heart. And as he stoops to pick it up, he thinks he hears the heart murmur, "My child, did you hurt yourself?"

Frankly, I can't handle this kind of God-love. Boiling it down to what I can handle is something like this: "You came to be, Kirk and Kyle, because I loved the man you call Daddy. I love you, not for what you do or don't do, but just because you're you. I'll always try to love you even when I'd like to send you back as factory rejects."

Taking it a step farther, God knows how to show his love. He knows how to give good gifts without spoiling us because he knows us so well he can tell the difference between what we need and what we want. He gives and gives and gives even when we don't appreciate it.

If I could understand this and get it across to my children with clarity, I could stop right here. I wouldn't have to resort to tiring speeches like, "How come I 'can't get no respect 'round here'? I sweat and slave and work all day, and no one, absolutely no one, appreciates me. I'm just another household word, a drudge."

Our Father disciplines us. Hebrews 12:6 assures us, "For those whom the Lord loves he disciplines." He doesn't pick on us for every little thing we do wrong, but only when we're way off base. It's his way of saying, "Son, you're headed for a heap of trouble."

The best discipline is that which leads children from outer controls to inner controls. Parents need to stand firmly behind their children with advice and guidance, but also learn to give them less and less as the need passes and as they learn to discipline themselves.

Proverbs 13:24 says, "He who spares his rod hates his son, but he who loves him disciplines him diligently." But hold on there! That doesn't mean discipline is to be used indiscriminately. You don't just whale away occasionally to cover all bases because you're sure that somebody's done something wrong at sometime, and if not today, tomorrow.

Constant punishment induces intimidation, humiliation, resentment, and eventually rebellion. Ephesians 6:4 reminds us, "Don't provoke your children to anger," even though my imperfect rule of thumb tends to be "Hit the first kid handy and ask questions later." The old Chinese proverb considers it more as a last resort: "He who strikes the first blow has run out of ideas."

God is wise and just, and his discipline always fits the disobedience. A butch haircut for the brand-new Barbie doll is not the same as shaving baby brother's head to see if he really does look like Yul Brynner.

Who's in charge? God doesn't worry about things like that. He knows who is. He doesn't need to cover up his own doubts like I do; he has no need to swagger around saying, "Come down off that roof right now, Buster. I don't care who your daddy is. I'm boss around here!"

Our Father frees us. He doesn't force us to do anything, but he gives us wiggling room. He knows this is how we grow to maturity. That doesn't mean we can jolly well do what we please, but he simply sets us free to respond.

This leads us to be responsible for our own actions. Then we can't blame God or anyone else. We can't say, "The devil made me do it"—he simply wanders in when we leave the screen door ajar.

God gives us freedom to have opinions that don't represent the management. And he doesn't even feel it necessary to pin a note to our jacket that says, "The opinions of this child are not necessarily those of his Father."

"You raise carrots, but you don't raise kids," Jess Lair says in a chapter title of his book *I Ain't Well—But I Sure Am Better.* He says being a parent is more like being their sponsor. That helps you to treat them as much like people as possible and as little like slaves and robots.

Instead of things to mold, our children are more like people to unfold. And to help them open up and blossom, one of our responsibilities is to educate them. Leo Buscaglia, associate professor of education at the University of Southern California, likens a parent as well as a teacher

The Gift of Children

to a guide. It's like this: There's a table full of wonder out there, and educating children is the process of leading them to it. You do all sorts of inviting things like decorating the table and preparing all the good food in the best way possible, but you can't make anybody eat. That's up to them.

Haim Ginott tells the story in *Teacher and Child* of a fire that broke out in a cramped attic. When the firemen rushed to put out the fire, they found a man who was heavily asleep. They tried to carry him downstairs but couldn't and were about to despair of saving him until the chief arrived. "Wake him up," he said, "and he'll save himself." [5]

It's our job to awaken our kids so they can save themselves. They can do it.

"Blessed is the family where children are allowed to become what they can as fast as they can," Charlie Shedd says in *You Can Be a Great Parent*. "Blessed also are the parents who, as fast as they can, will get out of the way." [6]

Our Father sets the perfect example. Someone has said we teach our children a little by what we say, a little more by what we do, but most of all by what we are. Whatever our children live with, that's what they are learning.

It's easy to yell, "If you don't learn to be more gentle with your baby brother, I'm gonna beat you to a bloody pulp." But it's harder to remember if there's something I want to change in my children, I'd better look first to myself. I must grow in order for my children to go through the proper stages of development.

My husband often says, "I don't practice what I preach, because I preach perfection from the Word, and God knows none of us can live up to that." Preachers have to be allowed that, but it's fatal for parents.

"Example," Albert Schweitzer said, "is not the main thing in influencing others. It is the only thing." [7] Children

145

have an uncanny ability to see through all the pretense and hypocrisy and masks that we wear. They grow up knowing us better than we know ourselves.

One of the stories my husband likes to tell to parents concerns a small boy who went to the zoo. He watched the ferocious antics of a couple of caged wildcats with great interest. Finally, he reached up and yanked the zookeeper's jacket and asked, "Say, mister, why are those cats so wild?"

"Well, son," he said, "I guess it's because their mother and daddy were wildcats."

Our Father inspires us. By giving a part of himself, his Spirit, he gives us the ability to be more than we would otherwise be. I could not tell you how he communicates it, but I know he does. It may be silent, but like sun shining on green pastures, it gives life and power.

In like manner, we "in-spirit" our children. We summon them to grow or diminish by how we make them feel. We constantly heal or destroy their inner being and send out powerful invitations to go forth or retreat. It's not so much in what we say to them, but what we whisper. It's not exactly what we do, but what they can see in us from moment to moment. It's how we encourage the smallest flicker of originality in them; hold out our hands to them or withhold them; or how we open up our warm hearts or keep them tightly closed. The process goes on all the time as we grieve with them when they're sad or rejoice in their smallest triumphs.

To the extent to which we shrink from life, we blight our children. We kill their dreams, paralyze their hopes, and cripple their joys. Their own gifts from God shrivel under our critical gaze, and their confidence vanishes as their achievements dwindle. Believing themselves less than they thought they were, they feel inadequate to face life and learn to operate at makeshift level, being ruled always by ought and should rather than by will or want. Their voices become echoes of people who just endure rather than enjoy.

On the other hand, when we open up our arms to life, we make them and everything in their lives more real. Our zest for life opens the door of wonder for them, and they grow up with the expectation that life is good, that other people are worth knowing and trusting, and it's great to be alive.

It's a call for authentic living, for living life to the limit; it's a voice whispering to us that we are a part of all that's good. People who have it know the secret of living in a small house while looking out on a large world.

This invitation to live is to see life as a voyage, not a harbor. It frees us to rise above any situation, any affliction, any limitation or cloud of despair, and then bloom as beautifully as anything made.

It means having the quiet certainty of the power of Jesus in our lives, that he is what gives them meaning and value. It's being able to declare with courage, "Even if I lose everyone I love and everything I have, I know I can make a life for myself, and it'll be a good one!" This attitude says, "I can't lose what is truly mine, and I can't lose that which doesn't belong to me in the first place."

For every door closed to me, God will open others. And when there doesn't seem to be even a tiny window opened to me, there is acceptance, knowing he will give me something even greater. It's letting angels go out so that archangels might come in.

There are no unimportant moments in our children's lives, and we are constantly making memories for them, as well as for ourselves.

Memories are easy to make: A dance in the warm rain or an overnight camping trip. A bowl of popcorn by the fire or blueberry-picking on the slopes of Mount Hood.

Will my sons only remember how busy I always was, and that I insisted that they spread up their bed each morning? I shudder to think of them remembering how jumpy I was when they wrestled in the middle of the living room floor. Or how furious I was when they tracked in mud on the shag carpets. Wouldn't it be horrible if my sons only remembered how I wouldn't let them clutter up the kitchen table with their model airplanes?

I hope they will remember me as one who often had both a smile and a tear, who liked to play as well as to pray, and as someone who was real.

But how do we let them go? Of all the events of life, children are the best indicators of how quickly time passes. They briefly dart through our lives and then disappear into adults. Only yesterday they wore training pants; today they stand taller than their father.

I'm no longer the mother of toddlers; Kirk is a teen and Kyle is twenty. Time runs short now, but I remember when it seemed forever. The children were always going through one stage or another, each one seeming to arrive a little before I'd grown accustomed to the last. I felt so tied down then, but now that I'm free, I've forgotten where it was I wanted to go, or what I wanted to do.

Soon both our sons will be gone, and then I can relax. My husband and I will be all that's left then. Just as it was in the beginning. My heart catches at the thought. No more muddy tennis shoes collecting at the front door; no more sticky handprints on the refrigerator door. The peanut butter and jelly jars will be tightly closed, and the towels will stay neatly folded on the racks.

Soon I will wonder as all parents eventually do: "Did it really happen? Were they ever so small and dependent or was it all a dream?" The day comes when some of the realities seem like dreams—the lost watch, the dirty

The Gift of Children

socks under the bed, the empty milk glasses by the phone. Even the wrecked Volkswagen which seemed so real at one time now seems like a dream.

We've always figured our boys were loaned to us for approximately eighteen years and regarded high school graduation as the day they'd leave us. They won't ever return after that, not really. They may be in and out from work and college, but it won't be the same.

Erma Bombeck once wrote a haunting story in her newspaper column "At Wit's End" about Mike, who, when he was three, wanted a sandbox in the yard which killed the grass. "It'll come back," his mother reassured his father. At five, he wanted a jungle gym, and then a plastic swimming pool. Later, there were campouts in a tent, a basketball hoop, and sleds. "It'll come back," the mother told the father each time. All the while, Mike's father shook his head and said, "I never asked for much in this life—only a patch of grass."

The article concluded with a report of the beautiful lawn they had that fall, where the gym shoes had trod and the bicycles used to lie. But Mike's father never saw it. He anxiously looked beyond the yard and asked with a catch in his voice, "He will come back, won't he?"

"I need more time," I told our older son, Kyle, during his senior year in high school. "There's so much more I wanted to give you, things I wanted you to know, experiences and memories I hoped we'd share before you left home." I'd always imagined his last years of high school would be different somehow, that we'd have a house big enough for a game room so he could have his friends in for Ping-Pong or pool. I'd hoped the family would have more leisure time and money for camping trips and vacations together.

He reminded me we'd bought the Ping-Pong table and stored it in the garage until we finally gave it away to the church to put in their gym. We'd taken some great camping trips, and once, a two-week vacation to Wyoming and Colorado. "And besides," he said with his quiet grin, "we've had lots of cross-country trips with the U-Haul moving van behind."

Like all new parents, we practiced on the first and supported our ignorance with good intentions and hope. All things considered, we proudly presented him to the world with no apologies (well, maybe just a few).

But time has already run out on us for him. He's been through a year and a half of college and a three-month tour of Europe. For the last few months, he's been home recovering from a near-fatal motorcycle accident that prematurely aged the whole family. These last few years, all in all, have been great when we could finally talk and laugh as person to person, not as parent to child. And it's been fun to be able to say to him, "I wish I'd had a friend like you when I was a teen."

Our other son, Kirk, is sixteen, only a few years beyond the caveman stage, and we've got a little more time with him. He's so intense about life, and, like most younger kids, he figures he has to work harder and run faster to catch up.

But in the time left with him, I have some plans too. I want to shed my myopic view of life and get rid of some of my rigidities and pomposity about adulthood. I want to call back the person who was once a kid herself. I want to enjoy the days I have left with him and recreate some of the carefree days before "duty" got hold of me.

It's too early to say how he's coming along. In the language of the recipe for boiling rice, he's in the simmer period of "no peeking." Take the lid off the pot too soon, and you're likely to be disappointed it's not done yet.

Eda LeShan, in *The Wonderful Crisis of Middle Age*, reminds us that ours is a generation of strange people. We aspire

The Gift of Children

to be perfect people and tend to feel guilty for the discontent and unfulfilled dreams of our mates, our children, and even our own parents. We find ourselves "caught in the middle, between our guilt as imperfect children and our guilt as imperfect parents."

"We are the first generation to blame ourselves for everything that ever went wrong with our children," she wrote. "We are the generation that were told we were responsible for the mental health—or lack of it—in our children. . . . Our parents—and all parents before them—assumed that if a child turned out peculiarly, it was a freak of nature; somewhere along the line he must have inherited 'bad blood' from an in-law. . . . Our ancestors were never burdened with the horrible idea that their attitudes, their childraising procedures, were in any way responsible for how their children turned out."[8]

> Help me, Lord, to make these last few years of parenting what I'll wish they had been. For once, make me that super-Mom, that all-weather person I've always yearned to be. Help me to round out their days in such a way that they'll always want to come back home to visit.
>
> And then help me to do the hardest of all: accept the kind of parent I've been even if I think I've messed things up. Where I've made mistakes, You make none. If I misunderstood, you understand. You can overrule all my failures and answer all my prayers. You can somehow make up for my lack.
>
> Free me from the guilt of not having perfect children. Help me to remember that I did what I thought was best and to know that I at least did the right thing instead of the wrong more than half the time.

I've taught them to be free, but how do I free myself of them? I found a way to cope with every stage somehow—I got through, didn't I?—but now how do I let them go?

Of course, they don't understand my reluctance to release them. They're excited and full of the juices of life. Life beckons to them, and they know they're ready for any kind of future. What they can't know yet is the bittersweet price of some of it. They fit Pearl S. Buck's description in *The Goddess Abides:* "The young do not know enough to be prudent, and therefore they attempt the impossible—and achieve it, generation after generation."

I wouldn't hold them even if I could, because I know their going is just as much a part of life as their coming. Perhaps it's more painful and harder than their birth because of the sadness at the end of any stage in life, that inevitable sense of loss. And I miss them even before they leave.

We can't keep our children forever except in our hearts and prayers. They'll not always live where we live or think as we think. We wouldn't want them to because this is what we've been striving for, to bring them into their own person. And when they leave, they are simply entrusted more completely back into the Father's care. No matter how much we love them, he loves them perfectly.

There comes the time to let them go. Tomorrow, when I have time, I can remember how it was. Then I hope to be one of those people who're having a grand time because their children are grown up.

In the meantime, may these words from an Argus poster give me parent power and sustain me:

"A prayer to be said when the world has gotten you down, and you feel rotten, and you're too doggone tired to pray, and you're in a big hurry and besides you're mad at everybody: Help."[9]

12.

The Gift of Power

This last gift is the power pack. It's really more of an empty box, and it's up to us to fill it. Without it, however, all of the other gifts only frustrate us.

Like most people, I know I have gifts but don't seem to be able to make the most of them. The use of my gifts is somehow always smaller than I thought it would be. As Herodotus of old said, "This is the bitterest pain among men, to have much knowledge but no power."

Power, in physics, means the rate of doing work. It involves such factors as force, distance, and time. The finding of new sources of power has been one of the key reasons for the progress of civilization. To increase the power of his own muscles, man has harnessed other forces and developed machines that use energy released by coal, gasoline, steam, electricity, atomic reaction, and so forth.

Because of this concept of physical power all around us, it's hard to understand the inner power Paul prayed for in Ephesians 3:16: ". . . to be strengthened with power through His Spirit in the inner man."

When we lived in Oregon, we liked to drive down the Columbia gorge to Multnomah Falls and stand at the bottom and watch the water cascade down the cliff. Occasionally, we'd drive up to Timberline Lodge and look out on Mt. Hood, the highest peak in Oregon. Like most people, we felt weak and awed when confronted with such majesty and power and beauty. Yet he who created all of these things also created us. And all the power of the falls and the majesty of all the mountains are part of the same life and power in us.

Ours is a power-conscious age. Some of us are concerned with horse power, black power, and woman power—while others seek some sort of inner power like will power or mind power.

We don't doubt that God is all-powerful, that he is "able to do exceeding abundantly beyond all that we ask or think." Or else, he wouldn't really be God. Most of us don't doubt that he can do anything at all, but we doubt if he does it for us. We're doubtful not about his power, but about his concern in our lives.

Manpower vs. Godpower. Actually, to a Christian, there's no such thing as manpower. Man has no power in and of himself; it's all from God. Unlike using the physical power around us, it's not a matter of harnessing a force and putting it to work by mechanical means, but more of a letting his Spirit work through us. Luke says it's a gift to those who ask: "If you then being evil, know how to give good gifts to your children, how much shall your Heavenly Father give the Holy Spirit to those who ask Him?"

The Gift of Power

Peter Marshall once prayed before the Senate, "Lord, give us help when we don't know what we ought to do. But give us a lot of help when we know very well what we ought to do, but we just don't want to do it."[1] And I might add, "Or when we seem unable to do it."

In thinking of the human characteristic to use force and to regard anything else as weakness, I recall an old episode in a TV program, "The Waltons." Though fictitious, I think it illustrates a profound truth. A high school class reunion was held at the Waltons' home, and at the conclusion of the dinner that night, one of the classmates made an informal speech. He was the most obviously successful man present as far as fame and wealth were concerned, and he spoke of his achievements as being mostly John Walton's fault. In their high school days together, he said, he was always running while John was always going past him at a walk. And over the years, while all the others had been wearing themselves to a frazzle, John had accumulated the things they'd all wanted—a family, love, peace, and joy. All the things they wanted from life, he'd got—"all while he was out walking."

We've all known someone like that. While we worked and sweated to gain wealth, honor, and possessions, he or she had achieved the real things we'd yearned for—while just "out walking."

Seed-growers and fruit-pickers. There's an old story that preachers like to tell about a man who dreamed he came to the great storehouse in which God keeps all the wonderful gifts he gives mankind. The man went up to the angel in charge and said, "All my life I've seen so much suffering and misery. I've seen wars, pestilence, and disease, and greed, hate, and envy. Please give me some love and joy and peace." The angel smiled and said, "I'm sorry, but we don't stock fruit—only seeds."

God gives us seeds in the form of all kinds of gifts. We provide the proper soil and the water and fertilizer, but we can't force the fruit to come.

When God gives us inner power to use our gifts, we know it by the fruit that his Spirit produces in our life. For some reason, however, the fruit of the Spirit mentioned in Galatians is often held up as a high achievement in Christian living. But when we turn fruit into fruits, plural, we create a legalistic trap, and the fruit eludes us. We think if we can somehow grit our teeth and learn how to love, then we can tackle joy; then on to peace, and so forth.

But Paul is saying that when, instead of you, the Spirit controls your life, he'll produce this fruit in you. Then he goes ahead to describe this fruit basket: it's love, joy, peace, patience, kindness, goodness, faithfulness, gentleness, and self-control.

The twilight zone. Having often lived in houses with few electric outlets, and all of them in the wrong places, my husband put an extra-long cord on my desk lamp. It drapes over the sofa, around the bookcase and table legs, and even then I have to gather it up with a big, thick rubber band. I've noticed that whenever there's an extra demand on the electricity in the house, the desk light dims. I don't understand how it diffuses the current to run it through such a long cord, but I know it does.

It occurs to me that this is what I do. I know the power of God is in me, but then I get all strung out and entangled and bunched up so that when there comes an extra demand on me, I am diminished. Instead of living my life to the limit, there are days when I seem powerless; when I'm caught in the twilight zone between shout and silence; when I endure, instead of enjoy. Circumstances in my life seem beyond my control, and I feel trapped by any and everything—my own sinful self, my family, inflation, the church, my job, my husband's job, and even the neighbor's kids. I build a wall around me, and then from my brick tomb of isolation and loneliness I agonize in bitterness and anger.

Dale Brown, family friend, tells me the British writer George MacDonald describes it something like this: He says we keep trying to build comfortable little bungalows of our lives. But when we invite the Lord in, he has a way of coming in and pushing out the walls until they come tumbling down. What he had in mind wasn't a dingy little hut, but more of a temple—or maybe a beautiful mansion with many rooms.[2]

Gimme, gimme, and gimme. I believe that God gives us what we need when we need it, and not what we want when we want it. And there's a big difference. He wants us to have power for abundant living; he offers it, but we don't avail ourselves of it. Is it possible we don't have more power because we haven't fully used the power we've already received? "Yet is every man his greatest enemy," said Sir Thomas Browne, "and, as it were, his own executioner."[3]

Do you ever notice our prayers? Much of the time it's not power we seek so much as removal of the problems in our lives. Instead of strength to face them and deal with them, we want them taken away. We pray for God to change our problems instead of changing us so that we can change the problems.

Phillips Brooks, a nineteenth-century clergyman, understood this when he wrote, "Do not pray for easy lives; pray to be stronger men. Do not pray for tasks equal to your powers; pray for powers equal to your tasks. Then the doing of your works shall be no miracle, but you shall be a miracle. Every day you shall wonder at yourself, at the richness of life which has come to you by the grace of God."[4]

The grace response. We've looked at just a few of the gifts God has given us. Now what does he want in return? He calls us from our potted-plant existence, where neither rain nor sun can reach us, to a kind of battlefront. While we'd like to work in our service after band practice and before scout meetings on Thursdays, he wants us as full-time volunteers. Paul said, "For by grace you have been saved through faith; and that not of yourselves, it is the gift of God; not as a result of works, that no one should boast. For we are His workmanship, created in Christ Jesus for good works, which God prepared beforehand, that we should walk in them" (Eph. 2:8–10).

What is the difference between the one- and the ten-talent person? Is it talent? Is it opportunity? Motivation? Could it be the measure of our ability to let the Lord supply the inner power? I know this: that of all the gifts God has given me, the gift of power is the one that I know the least about, and except for brief, glorious moments, the one I'm least able to use as he intends.

The Lord knows I'm not what I want to be. Indeed, all the things I'm not yet could fill another book. I've written these words, not because I consider myself an authority, but for opposite reasons.

I come out of a past and move toward a future. What I have right now is what God has given me, and what I do with it is my gift to him. I pray it will be more than it's been in the past, and more than I can possibly dream of in the future.

Whatever my gifts, I know that ". . . from everyone who has been given much shall much be required . . ." (Luke 12:48). Maranatha!

Notes

Chapter 1
1. John Powell, *The Secret of Staying in Love* (Niles, IL: Argus Communications, 1974), pp. 15–16.
2. Erich Fromm, *Escape from Freedom* (New York: Holt, Rinehart & Winston, 1963), pp. 116–17.
3. From an Argus poster; used by permission of Argus Communications, Niles, Illinois.
4. "Conformity Research: The Individual" in *Creativity and Conformity* (Ann Arbor, MI: Foundation for Research on Human Behavior, 1958), p. 15.
5. Some of these exercises are adapted from sessions of the Life-Planning Workshop, Kansas State University, Manhattan, KS, November 7, 1972.
6. Rainer Maria Rilke, *Letters to a Young Poet*, trans. M. D. Herter Norton (New York: W. W. Norton, 1934); excerpt used by permission.

Chapter 2
1. *Julius Caesar*, act 1, sc. 2, lines 140–41.
2. "Brain," *World Book Encyclopedia*, 1977.
3. Joseph Conrad, "Heart of Darkness," in *Youth and Two Other Stories*, 1902.
4. Emily and Ola d'Aulaire, "Put a Computer in Your Pocket," *Reader's Digest*, September 1975, pp. 115–18.
5. Alex F. Osborn, *Applied Imagination*, 3rd ed. rev. (New York: Charles Scribner's Sons, 1963), p. 128.
6. Elizabeth Allen Green, *What to Read Before College* (Cleveland: Case Western Reserve Press, 1971).

ALL THE THINGS YOU AREN'T . . . YET

7. *Writers at Work: The Paris Review Interviews,* vol. 4, ed. George Plimpton (New York: Viking Press, 1976), p. 19.
8. Norman Cousins, ed., "Advice to Unborn Novelists," *Writing for Love or Money* (London: Longmans, Green & Co., 1945), pp. 72–78.
9. *Macbeth,* act 4, sc. 1, line 14.
10. Lesley Conger, "Off the Cuff," *The Writer,* July 1972, p. 8.
11. Alexander Leaf, M. D., "Where Life Begins at 100," *Reader's Digest,* May 1973, pp. 158–62. (Condensed from *National Geographic,* January 1973.)
12. Edwin Diamond, "Can Exercise Improve Your Brain Power?" *Reader's Digest,* May 1973, pp. 101–104.
13. Don Bingham, "Man Alive: A Fitness Guide: Mental Quickness Can Be Maintained," *Register and Tribune* Syndicate, 1974.
14. Richard G. Case, "Intelligence-Sexuality Link Cited," Newhouse News Service, 1974.
15. Diamond, op. cit.

Chapter 3
1. Booker T. Washington, *Up from Slavery* (Garden City, NY: Doubleday & Co., 1963), p. 29.
2. Ralph Waldo Emerson, "Considerations by the Way," *Conduct of Life* (1860).
3. Arthur Koestler, *The Act of Creation* (New York: Macmillan, 1964).
4. Martin Buber, *Hasidism and Modern Man,* ed. and trans. Maurice Friedman (New York: Horizon Press, 1958), p. 139.

Chapter 4
1. W. E. Vine, *An Expository Dictionary of New Testament Words* (London: Oliphants, 1957), p. 115.
2. Blake Clark, "Nine Steps to a Longer Life," *Reader's Digest,* October 1970, pp. 84–87.
3. David Reuben, M. D., *The Save-Your-Life Diet* (New York: Random House, 1975). My summary statements of chapters 1–9.

Notes

4. Stuart Auerbach, "Live Clean, Live Long," *Los Angeles Times–Washington Post* News Service, 1975.
5. Clark, op. cit., p. 85.
6. Beverly Maurice, "A Smile on Your Face Does More Than You Think," *Houston Chronicle,* January 1975.
7. J. D. Ratcliff, "How to Avoid Harmful Stress," *Reader's Digest,* July 1970, pp. 79–82. (Condensed from *Today's Health,* American Medical Association, July 1970.)
8. "Coping with Stress," *Reader's Digest,* January 1974, pp. 117–20.
9. Alvin Toffler, *Future Shock* (New York: Bantam Books, 1971), p. 42.
10. John Schindler, M. D., *How to Live 365 Days a Year* (New York: Fawcett, Crest Books, 1968), p. xii.
11. Some of these ideas are suggested in chapter 11 of *A Farthing in Her Hand,* Helen Aldefer, ed. (Scottdale, PA: Herald Press, 1964).
12. Katherine Mansfield, *Bliss and Other Stories* (New York: Alfred A. Knopf, 1947).

Chapter 5
1. Bobbie Lee Holley, "God's Design: Woman's Dignity," Part II, *Mission,* vol. 8, no. 10, April 1975, p. 7.
2. Virginia Mollenkott, "The Total Submission Woman," *Christian Herald,* November 1975, pp. 26–30.
3. Ibid., p. 29.
4. Norman Parks, "Hearken, O Church!" *Integrity,* March 1975, p. 158.
5. Ibid., p. 156.
6. Dick Marcear, "What's Happening to Our Women?" *Central Herald,* vol. 12, no. 7, February 12, 1976, p. 2.
7. George Santayana, *The Life of Reason,* vol. 1 (1905–1906).
8. George Isaac Brown, *Human Teaching for Human Learning* (New York: Viking Press, 1971), pp. 12–13.
9. Jess Lair, *I Ain't Much, Baby . . . But I'm All I've Got* (Greenwich, CT: Fawcett, 1974), p. 213.
10. T. S. Eliot, "Little Gidding" in *Four Quartets* (New York: Harcourt Brace Jovanovich, Inc., 1943). Used by permission.

Chapter 6
1. John Kenneth Galbraith, *The Affluent Society* (New York: New American Library, 1958), p. 13.
2. "Still the Same Dream," *Houston Post*, September 7, 1975.
3. Booker T. Washington, *Up from Slavery*, p. 95.
4. Jess Lair, *I Ain't Well—But I Sure Am Better* (Garden City, NY: Doubleday, 1975), p. 195.
5. Ibid., p. 196.

Chapter 7
1. François, Duc de La Rochefoucauld, *Moral Maxims*, 1678.
2. Flannery O'Connor, *Mystery and Manners* (New York: Noonday Press, 1969), p. 159.
3. C. W. Skipper, "The Man Who Draws for Peanuts," telephone interview with Charles Schulz, *Houston Post*, January 9, 1976, p. 2E.
4. Lair, *I Ain't Much*, p. 210.
5. Alexander Solzhenitsyn, *The Gulag Archipelago* (New York: Harper & Row, 1974), p. 280.
6. William James, *The Will to Believe* (1897), p. 62.
7. Quoted in George Isaac Brown, *Human Teaching for Human Learning* (New York: Viking Press, 1971), p. 18.
8. Quoted in *Reader's Digest*, from Frances L. Brandon, *Bits and Pieces* (New York: Carlton Press).
9. Dale Wasserman and Joe Darian, *Man of La Mancha* (New York: Random House, 1966), p. 61.
10. Kahlil Gibran, *The Prophet* (New York: Alfred A. Knopf, 1923), p. 29. Used by permission.
11. Jess Lair, *I Ain't Much*, p. 242.
12. Eda LeShan, "Say 'Yes' to Life," *Woman's Day*, November 1970, pp. 51, 116, passim.

Chapter 8
1. *Houston Post* interview, Sunday, February 8, 1976.
2. Anne Morrow Lindbergh, *Gift from the Sea* (New York: Signet Books, 1955), p. 26.
3. Carol Kleiman, "Art of Assertion or Learning How to Say 'No,'" *Houston Post*, September 16, 1975.

Notes

4. Toffler, *Future Shock*, pp. 11, 19.
5. Jean Kerr, *Please Don't Eat the Daisies* (New York: Fawcett, 1959), p. 19.
6. Peter F. Drucker, *The Effective Executive* (New York: Harper & Row, 1967), pp. 23–24.
7. Alan Lakein, *How to Get Control of Your Time and Your Life* (New York: New American Library, Signet Books, 1973), p. 11.
8. Lair, *I Ain't Much*, p. 230.
9. Lair, *I Ain't Well*, p. 14.

Chapter 9

1. Dorothy Storck, "Fight the Aargh! in Life; Develop Your Own 'Space,'" Knight News Wire, in *Houston Post,* March 29, 1976.
2. Bobbie Lee Holley, *Person to Person* (Austin, TX: Sweet Publishing Co., 1969), p. 119.
3. Anne Morrow Lindbergh, *Locked Rooms and Open Doors* (New York: Harcourt Brace Jovanovich, 1974).
4. *Houston Chronicle,* May 2, 1975.
5. Lair, *I Ain't Well*, pp. 50–51.
6. Quoted in *Reader's Digest.*
7. Quoted in Holley, *Person to Person*, p. 27.
8. Dietrich Bonhoeffer, *Life Together* (New York: Harper & Row, 1954), p. 101.
9. Holley, *Person to Person*, p. 62.
10. Quoted from *Guideposts* in *Reader's Digest.*
11. Toffler, *Future Shock*, p. 93.
12. Ibid.
13. Alain Touraine, "Acceptance and Resistance," *Workers' Attitudes to Technical Change* (Paris: Organization for Economic Cooperation and Development, 1965), p. 95.
14. Donald C. Stewart, *The Authentic Voice* (Dubuque, IA: Wm. C. Brown Co., 1972), pp. 1, 2.
15. Lair, *I Ain't Much*, p. 45.
16. Quoted in *A Farthing in Her Hand*, p. 81.
17. John Powell, *Why Am I Afraid to Tell You Who I Am?* (Niles, IL: Argus Communications, 1969), p. 8.

18. Corrie ten Boom, *The Hiding Place* (New York: Bantam Books, 1974), p. viii.

Chapter 10
1. Mollenkott, "The Total Submission Woman," pp. 26–30.
2. Dr. Joyce Brothers, *The Brothers System for Liberated Love and Marriage* (New York: Peter H. Wyden, Inc., 1972).
3. Henri Nouwen. "The Gift of Solitude," *Faith/at/Work*, April 1976, p. 28.
4. Gabrielle Burton, *I'm Running Away from Home But I'm Not Allowed to Cross the Street* (New York: Avon Books, 1975).
5. Lindbergh, *Gift from the Sea*, p. 93.
6. Gibran, *The Prophet*, p. 13. Used by permission.
7. Clare Booth Luce, "Can Marriage Be Happy?" *Reader's Digest*, April 1975, pp. 81–87. (Condensed from *Bulletin* of the Baldwin School, Bryn Mawr, PA, September 1974.)
8. Helen B. Andelin, *Fascinating Womanhood* (Santa Barbara, CA: Pacific Press, 1963), pp. 23, 182.
9. Jim Reynolds, *Secrets of Eden: God and Human Sexuality* (Austin, TX: Sweet Publishing Co., 1975), p. 17.
10. Rollo May, *Love and Will* (New York: W. W. Norton, 1969), p. 39.
11. Lair, *I Ain't Well*, pp. 108–109, 113.
12. Norman Lobsenz, "How Husbands Feel about Working Wives," *Woman's Day*, July 1976.
13. Walter Trobisch, *Love Is a Feeling to Be Learned* (Downers Grove, IL: Inter-Varsity Press, 1972), p. 12.
14. Lindbergh, *Gift from the Sea*, p. 106.

Chapter 11
1. Charlie W. Shedd, *You Can Be a Great Parent* (Waco, TX: Word Books, 1970), p. 7.
2. Kerr, *Please Don't Eat the Daisies*, p. 15.
3. Quoted in *Reader's Digest*, as submitted by Phyllis Battelle, King Features.
4. Holley, *Person to Person*, p. 30.
5. Haim Ginott, *Teacher and Child* (New York: Macmillan, 1972), p. 256.

Notes

6. Shedd, *You Can Be a Great Parent*, p. 20.
7. "Quotable Quotes," *Reader's Digest*.
8. Eda LeShan, *The Wonderful Crisis of Middle Age* (New York: Warner Communications, 1975), pp. 31, 32.
9. Used by permission of Argus Communications.

Chapter 12
1. *Mr. Jones, Meet the Master* (London: Revell, 1950), p. 128.
2. Quoted in C. S. Lewis, *Mere Christianity* (New York: Macmillan Publishing Co., Macmillan Paperbacks, 1978), p. 174.
3. Sir Thomas Browne, *Religio Medici* (1642), pt. 2, sec. 4.
4. Phillips Brooks, *Sermons Going Up to Jerusalem*.